Is Your Family Driving You Mad?

Is Your Family Driving You Mad?

Anne Nicholls

PIATKUS

Visit the Piatkus website!

Piatkus publishes a wide range of bestselling fiction and
non-fiction, including books on health, mind, body & spirit,
sex, self-help, cookery, biography and the paranormal.

If you want to:
- read descriptions of our popular titles
- buy our books over the internet
- take advantage of our special offers
- enter our monthly competition
- learn more about your favourite Piatkus authors

VISIT OUR WEBSITE AT: www.piatkus.co.uk

Copyright © 2004 by Anne Nicholls

First published in Great Britain in 2004 by
Piatkus Books Ltd
5 Windmill Street
London W1T 2JA
e-mail: info@piatkus.co.uk

The moral right of the author has been asserted

A catalogue record for this book is
available from the British Library

ISBN 0 7499 2509 4

Set in New Baskerville by Palimpsest Book
Production Limited, Polmont, Stirlingshire

Printed and bound by
Legoprint SpA, Italy

Reading this book will give you more under-standing of how your family ticks, as well as lots of down-to-earth tips on how to cope with everyday issues such as crossed wires and sibling rivalries. After reading, keep it on the shelf. Life being life, there will always be someone in need of the author's compassionate wisdom.

– Gael Lindenfield

Also by the Author

Make Love Work For You

To all my family, especially:

Mick and Paddy Booth
John, Sheila and Alan Booth
Janet Calderwood, Anna and Elaine Kennedy
My husband Stan Nicholls
And my wonderful daughter Marianne Gay

Acknowledgements

Thanks as ever to Ian Stewart and Adrienne Lee of the Berne Institute and John Monk-Steel; Tony Tilney for his insightful and supportive supervision; Elizabeth Doggart for exciting opportunities (and parties); and to Marilyn Wright and Tricia White for their support.

Thanks also to the people at Piatkus, especially Penny Phillips for her caring input, and Jana Sommerlad and Paola Ehrlich for all their hard work.

And to Laura Longrigg, agent supreme.

Contents

Introduction

Do you want more confidence and better relationships with your family?

What do you want in a book about families? *How tos* for making your family life less of a battlefield and more like a place to share fun? Ways of unshackling yourself from the pain of the past so you can launch yourself confidently into the future?

Is Your Family Driving You Mad? is designed to help you do both these things. It's about finding and nurturing the seeds of self-belief rooted in your origins so you can live a fuller, richer life. When you believe in yourself you can deal more effectively with life's ups and downs in every area from work to leisure and love.

It's also about learning to build closer ties with the people around you and still stay safe. Wouldn't you love to have a family and a home that takes you to its heart when you need a refuge and gives you a springboard when it's time to take wing? A place that feels like a warm, glowing hearth on a cold, dark night? A group of people who are cheering you on and delighting in your good fortune?

With a healthy take on yourself and your family, you can help your children be happier individuals who negotiate the jagged reefs of adolescence with less friction all around. You can also have a more rewarding way of dealing with your relatives and the rest of the world. As you grow your sense of personal worth and power, you and those you're connected to can enjoy a deeper, truer affection. Wouldn't you like to set acceptable limits so you don't get swamped by other people's moods or needs? Or to become more truly and wonderfully your own unique self? Don't you want to move more hopefully along a path that leads to the desires of your own heart?

You may doubt that these inspirational ideas are possible for you, but they could be. You'll never know unless you give them your best shot. They're not rocket science. They're down-to-earth, practical solutions to everyday situations. Hundreds of thousands of people all around the globe are living these dreams right now. They're improving their careers, revitalising relationships that used to be stale or frustrating and taking pleasure in their family life where once they would have thought it an unattainable fantasy.

It's not because they were born lucky. Sadly, for many of us learning only comes out of pain. If you had a difficult time growing up there's a chance you might be scared of any changes in case they make things worse. But changes can be good as well as bad, and happiness doesn't have an on/off switch. Inch by inch and step by step you can make the changes you need to become happier.

One of the good things about working from a book like this is that you're in control. You can take the ideas you're ready for, work at your own pace and move on when you feel the time is right. You will gradually find that the world becomes a brighter place. Even those in the most dire circumstances can find positive ways of facing their problems.

Whether you grew up with them or not, mothers and fathers, brothers and sisters, aunts and uncles, and cousins and grand-parents are part of the jigsaw that made up your childhood world. For some, the absence of these people in their lives was a crucial factor. For others, what their relatives did formed part of the mould into which they had to fit in order to survive. Whether we're talking about biological, foster, step or adoptive families, how you saw yourself in relation to the people around you became a sketch – incomplete, pencilled in, rubbed out and inked over, but a sketch nonetheless – of how you've come to see yourself in your world right now. Like artists who can paint over a few half-formed outlines to produce a beautiful landscape, people too can redraw themselves if they want to.

It's not about blame. You're not responsible for the hand you were dealt in life – but you can learn to take responsibility for how you play it. That way you can start to build up more happiness, better relationships, more confidence, more success – if that's what you want. Once you leave childhood behind, you're the one who's in charge of your life. If you want to make life better for yourself, even if that means bearing up under tragic circumstances, this book is for *you*.

Is Your Family Driving You Mad? isn't a substitute for therapy. If you feel your problems are so deep you could go crazy – that you could hurt yourself or someone else – it's a good idea to seek help from your doctor or a counsellor right away. This book will still be here waiting for you when you're ready.

Is Your Family Driving You Mad? is based on therapeutic principles that are used all over the world. You don't, however, have to have any technical knowledge to enjoy the book and get something useful out of it. I have included true-life stories showing how people like you have solved problems like yours. Not exactly the same, of course, because everyone's problems are specific to them. But anyone who's ever been lonely, had self-doubts or found themselves with a broken heart or a shattered dream will recognise something that strikes a chord – and that's all of us, however successful (or overwhelmed) we feel right now.

Is Your Family Driving You Mad? therefore covers two themes that intertwine: you and the people who are supposed to be closest to you: your family. Finding ways to deal constructively with what hurt you in the family of your childhood not only gives you more confidence and more choices, but also provides you with tools for making life with partners, children and step-children more comfortable all around. There are ideas for improving your relationships with your brothers, sisters and parents as you and they grow older.

   A word about family life. It isn't set in stone. In some ways it's changed more over the last half-century than ever before. Fewer children now grow up in the traditional mother-and-father home. Some people grow up with one parent, others with none. Sometimes parents bring children from previous relationships into existing families, so that families are blended. I use the word *parent* to mean someone who takes responsibility for a child's welfare regardless of whether the child is his or her biological offspring. Children may grow up with gay parents, in a children's home, or with adoptive parents or foster carers. Some communities bring up all their children in a new form of extended family.

The old rules are breaking down. Even when they were generally supposed to work there were plenty of families where one or more members didn't feel good a lot of the time. In 99 per cent of cases parents do their best, but circumstances are often against them in one way or another. Individuals can't always live together in total harmony. One person's desire can be another's nightmare. Sometimes there just isn't enough of something to go around. In any family set-up it's not hard to feel lonely or frustrated at least some of the time.

We've all emerged out of this random cocktail of social, genetic and personal factors. Once you leave the family you grew up in, you have the chance to look around and make new choices in relation to yourself and the way you're going to relate to other people. With greater self-knowledge and improved people skills, you'll find it easier to overcome obstacles. A wider, brighter horizon awaits you.

Is Your Family Driving You Mad? can help you on your way. To all who read this book, whether that's in pain, hope or simply interest, I wish you the empowerment and happiness you seek.

Part I

From a Child's Point of View

We all of us start life as children. Think back for a moment. Can you remember what it was like when you couldn't reach the door knob? When your parents could pick you up bodily and move you from one place to another? When they could smack you and tell you off? When you had no say about your bedtime hours or what you ate? Even if you can't remember a thing before the age of eight or nine, you've probably got strong feelings about the big, strong people who brought you up.

This means everyone starts life feeling smaller and less powerful than others. Of course, you'll have updated this view in many ways, but some aspects of it might be so painful and seem so inevitably true that you don't want to think about them, let alone dare to challenge them even as an adult. This might show as shyness, unhealthy relationships, stress, workaholism, you name it. The way you've always seen yourself might limit your confidence, your choices and your potential for happiness.

This section is about updating damaging old beliefs. It's not a question of blaming yourself or your parents, just about making new decisions with all your current abilities. Then you'll be able to develop a good sense of self-worth in every aspect of your life. If you'd like to, you can also transform your relationships with your family. You'll find that many of the techniques I show with one set of family members work just as well with others. Good luck!

Chapter 1

Transforming Your Life Position

Have you ever felt as though you're not good enough? Here's how you can start seeing yourself and your family of origin in a different light and transform your Life Position.

What have I done to deserve this?

In my consulting room **Adam** furiously winked away tears as he burst out, 'Why can't things ever go right for me? Other people sail through life. Why can't I? What's wrong with me?'

At some point or another you've probably said the same thing. I know I used to. Believing that there's something wrong with you, that if you dare to be happy something horrible will happen to spoil it, is pretty common. Hospital staff frequently hear patients or relatives cry out in despair, 'Why me? What have I done to deserve this?' as though accidents and illness only happen to the wicked.

For thousands of people, everyday life teeters insecurely on such scary beliefs, as though there were a hammer over their heads just waiting to fall. Here are examples of just a few of the sentiments expressed by these people.

- I'm not worthy so if I'm not careful I'll be found out.
- People just don't like me.
- Some people can have great jobs but I can't.
- I'd better hang on to my miserable relationship and dreary family life or I'm doomed to an echoingly empty future.
- I can't expect anything better.

If you know the misery of such beliefs, whether you find life humdrum or terrifying, the thought of making changes probably seems either threatening or impossible. But it needn't be. Let's see how Adam got into the fix that brought him to counselling and what it had to do with family life. Could he learn to overcome the problems besetting him? And could this help you?

Adam's Life Position

As he sat in the consulting room, Adam looked grey and drawn. Worry etched his face and his shoulders were tense. He held one hand across his stomach, trying to ease the pain of his ulcer as he explained what had happened.

Adam is a senior social worker and one of his trainees had made an emergency hardship payment from the wrong fund and with the wrong paperwork. Adam felt guilty because he was responsible for his trainee, so he tried to sort out this innocent mistake without his line manager discovering it. Unfortunately, the tangled paper trail was spotted in a snap inspection and he was actually caught 'red-handed' putting the money back from his own pocket. He was accused of embezzlement and suspended until a tribunal could be held.

Racked with shame, Adam felt powerless and afraid. What if he lost his job? His pension? His house? What if he was branded a criminal and sent to jail? Nothing his wife and children said could cheer him up. Slumped in his armchair at home, he hid from the world. Then his father, a vicar, rang to give his view: 'There's no smoke without fire,' he said. For Adam, this was the final straw. It was then that the pain of a stomach ulcer drove him to the doctor, who persuaded him to come for counselling.

As Adam began to move through the process of therapy, he discovered that he was acting out a set of beliefs about himself and other people: his basic Life Position. Sometimes these beliefs shifted under the pressure of external events but generally he returned to his 'home' position. It can be described like this: *There's something wrong with me. Other people can cope but I can't. Even when things are going well I'm bound to slip up and then everyone will know . . .* Just what it was they'd know depended on circumstance. At different times Adam might finish that sentence with: 'I'm not good enough', 'I'm not clever enough' or 'what a failure I am'.

Because Adam thought 'everyone' would be judging him, he also believed that 'everyone' was smarter than he was (or they wouldn't be able to catch him out) and more powerful than he was (because he was afraid there'd be dire consequences when 'everyone' found out the 'terrible truth' about him). The present circumstances, underlined by his father's doubts, seemed to confirm his gloomy world view.

Of course it's easy to see from the outside that the truth about Adam wasn't terrible at all. The trainee had explained how she'd unwittingly caused the whole situation. Besides, Adam had an exemplary record. His colleagues would vouch that he was honest to the core. His wife and children still loved him and believed him, and if necessary there were other jobs. Even his boss said the tribunal would be nothing more than a slap on the wrist. But from the inside, Adam felt well and truly doomed. A lot of people feel that way at some time or another. Have you? Did it make things seem better or worse?

The first step to changing things for the better is finding out how you got where you are. If you're beginning to wonder whether you too have unconsciously held yourself in a painful Life Position, read on. You'll see that you're not alone – and that you *can* start to make life better.

What Life Positions are there?
Since Life Positions (or life beliefs) are about yourself in relation to other people, you can sum them up with combinations of *I* and *You*. See if you can recognise any of the Life Positions discussed below in yourself.

I-U+
Adam's Life Position had himself as less powerful and worthy than others, so it can be represented as **I** with a minus (-) sign after it, and **You** followed by a plus (+) sign. In an attempt to make up for his perceived inadequacy, Adam constantly struggled to do everything perfectly. Then he'd feel pressured and work even harder to compensate. His workaholism caused tensions with his family and

his perception of disgrace stirred up his ulcer. These are common side effects of I-U+ beliefs. There will be more on how Adam recovered further on. First let's look at the other Life Positions.

- **I-U-: I'm not OK and neither are you.** People with this as their basic Life Position often feel they can't cope. They think others won't help and might even make things worse. Their belief is that it'll all go horribly wrong – so what's the point? The best they can hope for is not to be noticed.
- **I+U-: I'm OK but you're not.** From this Life Position people don't suffer fools gladly. They may get angry and impatient or become martyrs to 'make' others feel bad. They're likely to behave in ways that leave them feeling lonely and unappreciated.
- **I+U+: I'm OK and so are you.** This is the healthy view. People with this Life Position accept themselves and get on with what they have to do. They forgive themselves and others for mistakes, trusting that generally other people will treat them fairly. They're confident socially and are more likely to feel happy and fulfilled.

Of course, all of us slip in and out of the various Life Positions according to what's happening in our lives. You're more likely to enjoy the I+U+ position if you've just won the lottery than if your car's broken down in a thunderstorm, but usually you'll have a 'home' position too. Can you identify yours?

Conditional Acceptability
Given that people often don't believe they're acceptable as they are, they may try and save themselves from their painful Life Position with a get-out clause. These are beliefs like:

- I'm OK if I do everything perfectly.
- I'm OK if I don't let others know how I'm feeling.
- I'm OK if I look as though I'm trying hard because then someone will rescue me.
- I'm OK if I please other people.
- I'm OK if I do a lot of things at top speed.

These five beliefs can trigger automatic behaviours that you'll almost certainly recognise in yourself and others. They show most clearly when you're under pressure. Think back to the last time you were in a panic or having an argument. How did you feel about your family, your colleagues, your friends? Did you think you were as important, as powerful or as capable as they were? Did you feel able to ask for help if you needed to? Or did you sell yourself short, forget what you wanted to say, blush and stammer, or keep your opinions to yourself? Did you placate other people? Did you lash out and then feel a fool for losing your temper? Or maybe you went through a moment of despair before throwing yourself even harder into work?

Which of these five beliefs did you show first? Did you show another one second? How do you feel about it now? And are you willing to start learning that you matter as much as anyone else? If any of these old beliefs ring true for you, read on. Throughout this book you'll find ways of protecting yourself from painful fears so that you can build a new, positive belief in your own acceptability.

The transmitted world

You can see that the beliefs that drove Adam's behaviour were: 'I'm OK if I do everything perfectly and I'm OK if I don't let others know how I'm feeling'. But however hard he tried to hide what he saw as his shameful inadequacy, *they* knew. Now Adam felt physically as well as emotionally handicapped. He spent the empty days listlessly, too sick at heart to be seen in public. Why did Adam respond in this way? Where did these damaging beliefs come from?

Although Adam was in his fifties, he recognised his beliefs as having been there as long as he could remember. When he was growing up, as all children do he developed what seemed to be a blueprint to guide him through life. His father was a vicar, remote and strict, and his mother was busy with parish duties and housework. Here are just a few of the perfectly ordinary rules his parents imposed. Underneath each one you'll find the decisions young Adam made in response.

Don't make a noise because it will disturb Daddy.
I'm not as important as other people. I'm a nuisance. I can't have fun and I can't have friends. I'm in the way so I shouldn't be here at all.

Don't cry. Be a brave little soldier.
I'm wrong to feel hurt or sad. I must pretend I don't feel what I feel.

Don't answer back. Daddy knows best.
What I think or feel doesn't count. I can't make good decisions.

Get good marks at school so you can be a vicar too when you grow up.
Daddy's good and he's a vicar. I don't want to be one so I'm not good. I don't get good grades so I'm a failure.

From an outside, adult point of view you can see that the messages Adam took in weren't what his parents were sending. His mother and father were good, caring people who expected Adam to know that they loved him and wanted him to grow up happy, safe and valued. They would have been mortified if they'd realised how lonely and unwanted he felt.

Back then, however, Adam was only able to use the limited thinking skills of a child. That's a bit like wearing blinkers so you don't see the full picture. You've believed that certain parts of the picture aren't there so you respond to the incomplete version. As he grew up with these blinkers, Adam continued to miss bits of data that might have allowed him to update his view of himself and the world. He interpreted parts of what he did see as confirming his lack of worth. For example, when he excitedly wanted his mother to admire a picture he'd painted, she might say, 'In a minute, dear. Mummy's making supper right now.' She probably meant something like, 'Adam mustn't come near the cooker because I love him and I don't want him to get burnt,' but what he heard was *I'm not important. Mummy doesn't want to be close to me. Even my best isn't good enough. I have to be absolutely perfect to try and get her approval.* When you add some of the other messages he'd internalised, the ones that said, *I'm wrong to feel hurt or sad. I must pretend I don't feel what I feel. I'm a nuisance,* you can see why little Adam didn't feel able to ask his mother for reassurance.

Bringing the transmitted world into the present

The world that had unwittingly been transmitted to Adam in his childhood seemed hostile and he was apparently powerless in it. Now, in therapy, he started to see how he'd been acting out his I-U+ Life Position in his present situation.

When his junior at work made the mistake, Adam did his best to smooth it over without anyone finding out he hadn't given her the guidance she needed. *(Even my best isn't good enough. I can't make good decisions. I'm a failure.)* When it came to light, Adam's worst fears seemed to be confirmed: *they*, his powerful bosses and colleagues, had found out that he wasn't good enough. He did little to defend himself because he believed he had no power to make them change their minds. *(I'm not as important as other people. I'm a nuisance.)* Far from telling his rigid father how he felt about his unjust accusation, Adam meekly accepted the criticism, then hid away so no one would know how bad he felt. *(What I think or feel doesn't count. I must pretend I don't feel what I feel.)*

I don't know about you, but I don't think I've ever met anyone who hasn't experienced such hurtful, self-limiting beliefs at least some of the time. But what if Adam realised he was no longer a child at everyone's mercy but an adult with power of his own? How could he do things differently and get a better outcome? Could you learn to do the same?

Rewriting the present

Like most of us, Adam had tried to bury his old beliefs because they were so painful. They lurked in the back of his mind, just waiting to pounce. Logic helped a bit: he might be exonerated, there were other jobs anyway, and his wife and kids still loved him. Nevertheless, this rational approach scarcely dented his fears. He felt dreadful. What he needed was a way of updating his beliefs on the feelings level.

I invited Adam to imagine his father not as the stern adult but as a child of around seven, with muddy knees and jam around his mouth, who made messes and sometimes made mistakes.

Could he imagine himself as an adult asking his father as such a child, 'Do you always do everything perfectly?' This works for many clients, but Adam said flatly, 'Impossible. Too scary.'

All right then. What if Adam imagined his grandfather, an even more remote and austere figure, asking Adam's father why he had mud on his knees and jam around his mouth? That was possible. If necessary, Adam could have imagined his grandfather as a cartoon giant and his father as a cartoon child. Adam's austere grandfather asked the smaller figure of the father-child, 'Are you always perfect?' and back came the answer: no.

'Are you all-powerful?' asked Grandfather.

'No,' said the little boy.

'Do you sometimes get blamed for things that aren't your fault?'

'Yes,' the boy said indignantly. 'It's not fair!'

'Do you like it when people disregard your feelings?'

'No! I hate it when they won't listen to me.'

Now Grandfather asked, 'When you grow up, would you want your son to be treated unfairly?'

'No.'

'Do you want him to be unhappy?'

'No,' said the boy-child.

'To have his feelings disregarded?'

'No.'

'Would you want him to stand up for himself?'

'Yes I would! I hope he does!'

In the counselling room Adam was now crying with relief. Still in his imagination, he thanked his grandfather and the boy his father had been. Then he said aloud the permissions he'd now taken in: 'I am as important as other people. I can stand up for myself. My feelings count. I can be happy.'

Adam now anchored these permissions in the present by working out how he would act on them. This included getting a lawyer to represent him at the tribunal. Just as importantly, he came up with some ideas for enjoying his unexpected holiday. He had always dreamed of playing in a band – an idea he'd given up in his teens when his father disapproved – so he began guitar lessons.

And the tribunal, of course, cleared everything up with only a reprimand. It didn't matter. He'd already decided to be less critical of his staff and more approachable towards them. Moreover, he wrote a polite but assertive letter saying how hurt he was that his father had automatically assumed Adam was guilty of embezzlement. Adam was surprised but delighted when his father phoned to apologise for his misjudgement.

Bringing your positive new beliefs into your life

If you have believed that you too are only conditionally acceptable, you might find the idea of your true acceptability challenging. Some of you might even find it scary. That doesn't mean you'll always think it's scary. You've managed to survive with those negative thoughts this far, so congratulations! When you're ready you can begin to change those beliefs to more postive, self-supportive ones at your own pace.

Here are some ways of moving towards acceptance of yourself as a worthwhile human being. Please read through to the end of the chapter and then come back to do the exercise if you're willing. If you feel safe doing so, why not try saying the following sentences aloud and see how you react inside?

- It's OK to be myself. No one's perfect so I don't have to be perfect either.
- My feelings are important to me because they affect what I do. I can respect my feelings as much as other people's.
- I can do my best and ask outright for help if I want it.
- I'm allowed to rest as well as work.
- I can't please everyone. I can respect my own wishes as well as other people's.

If you feel comfortable saying these sentences, great! You can say them over and over to help drown out any negative conditioning you've acquired over the years. If you feel discomfort, confusion or fear, you could try adding some of these 'softeners' at the beginning and see if that works for you.

- I am starting to know that . . .
- I am now learning to accept that . . .
- I am willing to want to learn to accept that . . .

Should you still feel apprehensive about applying these new beliefs to yourself, the upside is that you now have information on what you might want to address when you're ready. You won't be the only person in this situation, and you have my sympathy. As you read through this book, why not come back to this section from time to time to see whether you now feel safe enough to take in these positive messages? If you need help in accepting them, you're allowed to ask for it. Therapists, friends, family and religious leaders are some of the people who could help you.

SUMMARY

If you have recognised any of these painful beliefs, are you willing to update them? Will you, in your imagination, create a scene where the authority figures from your past are cut down to size in a human and caring way? Will you start to recognise that you, and your feelings, matter as much as other people's? I hope so!

Chapter 2

Editing Your Life Script

Has it seemed as though you're stuck? That you'll never be good enough for other people? Now you can rewrite your life story to find more fulfilment and appreciation.

Do you feel stuck?

Heather came to therapy after her third divorce. She sobbed, 'It's me, isn't it? My last husband was right. I'm ugly, fat, stupid and worthless and now I'm old. That's why this always happens to me, isn't it?'

Yet Heather was quite pretty, curvaceous and attractively dressed. Between her first and second marriages she'd been a librarian and there was nothing wrong with her intelligence. She was in her late thirties, which meant she was probably less than half-way through her life. All the same, between believing she was powerless to do anything different and blaming men for 'always' treating her badly, she felt stuck, with a lonely old age looming over her.

Lots of people come to therapy because of that energy-sapping, hope-devouring feeling of being stuck. Other people's ideas seem to confirm their 'stuckness'. You've seen how Heather fell for her husband's verbal abuse.

If you too have felt stuck, unable to live up to your own or others' expectations, wouldn't you like to free yourself and get a happier outcome?

Life Scripts

Heather began by identifying her Life Script. Everyone has their own unique way of living out their original Life Position. It's as if they are living in a film that's heading for a certain conclusion. Even if it's an unpleasant ending they don't know how to change it. You could say they're stuck in a script.

Everyone's script is unique to them. In some areas you might be a winner, in others a plodder and in some a loser. Script is about beliefs that seem automatic, pre-programmed and inevitable. These beliefs block out selected parts of your awareness but leave you free to respond appropriately in other areas.

As an example, Heather had decided she was no good at sports but good at reading, cookery and needlework (so which of these things did she practise to improve and which did she avoid?); that she'd never be a high earner (so she didn't bother learning business skills); that boys were more important than girls (so she was shy and couldn't disagree with men) and that being married was the only real form of validation for women. This meant she'd put up with years of physical and emotional abuse, and now, divorced again, she was terrified of spending the rest of her life alone. There are certainly degrees of winning and of losing:

- With the **first degree** of losing you might just be fed up. Maybe you put a brave face on things or have a good moan with the people around you, but you still feel stuck.
- With the **second degree**, things are bad enough that you're reluctant to talk about them with friends or family. The problems could involve trouble with the law, a traumatic relationship breakdown, severe problems with work, or brief hospitalisation for depression or anxiety.
- The **third degree** can, literally, be fatal unless you change it. It might involve physical harm to yourself or others; repeated hospitalisation for emotional or health problems; a jail sentence; an inability to hold down a job; or public disgrace. As with classical tragedies, the seeds of the final disaster can be traced back to some early decision about life, other people and yourself. Think of Romeo and Juliet, or Julius Caesar.

Meanwhile other people just plod along living banal lives, neither spectacularly successful nor spectacularly failing, not particularly happy or sad, just middle of the road.

Then there are the winners. They might not be seen as winners by other people but they've achieved their own goals and are comfortable with that. If you've made a fortune but lost your health and your friends in the process, you're not a winner. If you're scraping a living on a subsistence farm and enjoying it, you're a winner whether others think so or not. The casting vote in whether you're a winner, a plodder or a loser is your own.

There are other influences. Accidents do happen. A happy, successful person can be mown down by a runaway truck. It's certainly harder to be an athlete or an artist if you're missing your hands or feet, but it is possible. If your upbringing didn't teach you how to manage money or relationships successfully, you can find out how to do so – but only if you learn new skills and apply them.

How does all this relate to Heather and her unhappy relation-ship history? Could examining your own history in a new way help you rewrite your Life Script too?

Where do Life Scripts come from?

Picture Heather, aged four, standing on the window-seat with her mother's arms around her. The two of them are waiting for her father to come home. Her mother is trying to keep up Heather's spirits by pretending she's neither unhappy nor worried because her father is late again. Eventually her mother says, 'It's no good. You'll have to go to bed or you'll be tired in the morning.' Just then the father's car skids into the drive. Heather's bedtime is forgotten as she and her mother race to the front door. Her father staggers in and her mother shouts, 'Ray! Where have you been? I've been worried out of my mind!'

The father scoops up Heather, saying, 'Working to keep you, where do you think? Give Daddy a love, Heather. At least one of my girls is glad to see me.' He slobbers beery kisses over his daughter and snaps, 'Come on, Vera! I'm starving. I want my dinner on the table in five minutes. It's not as if you've had anything else to do today.'

Tight-lipped, the mother goes out to the kitchen. The father carries Heather into the living-room and turns on the TV. He sits down with his daughter on his lap and watches the news. Heather thinks he smells bad and his bristles scratch but she won't anger him by saying so. When she tries to tell him about her friend's new puppy, he shushes her. She tries to squirm away but his grasp tightens. Heather wriggles harder. Suddenly her father gets cross and pushes her roughly onto the floor.

Heather tries not to cry. Her father says nastily, 'I did bring a present home for my good girl but I'm not giving it to a cry-baby.' It's even harder not to cry when her mother brings her father's dinner through and he says, 'Can't you stop this brat whining, Vera? Shouldn't you have put her to bed by now?'

'I'm sorry, dear,' her mother says anxiously, putting the blame firmly on Heather by adding, 'She wouldn't go to bed until she'd seen you.' The father grunts and starts eating while the mother rushes Heather upstairs. Later, in bed, Heather hears her mother laughing at her father's jokes. She falls asleep thinking, 'Daddy's lovely sometimes.' Sure enough, when she wakes up, he's left a bag of sweeties for her.

This is just one scene from Heather's childhood. It mirrors many memories and contrasts with others, but the common threads were that happiness and acceptance depended on her father's moods and the consequent need to placate him.

What decisions did little Heather make with her childhood thinking? Here are some of them. Can you see what elements of this scene led her to these conclusions?

About people:
- Men are always like Dad and women are like Mum.
- Men are more important than women. Their feelings always come first.
- Women have to please men. Their feelings don't count and must be hidden.
- Men earn the money so women have to look after them to survive.
- Only having a man really makes proper women happy.
- Only having a man gives proper women status.

- Men behave arbitrarily so women probably don't end up that happy anyway.
- There's nothing women can do about it.

About herself:
- I'll learn domestic skills so I won't end up alone.
- I'm OK if I try hard to please men (even if they're grouchy).
- Whatever I do is probably not good enough.
- My feelings don't count but I'll be OK if I look as though I'm happy.
- I'm not important.
- All marriages are like this so if other people are happy, I'm doing something wrong.
- If I don't please my man I'm a worthless failure.

Heather developed these invalid beliefs because they seemed to fit what was happening in her family. They certainly shaped the lifestyle her parents modelled, and together with the I-U+ Life Position Heather developed, they formed the outline for her script. As she grew up and met other viewpoints, she tended to ignore or reject the ones that didn't fit with all this while remembering incidents like her husbands' abuse that confirmed her world-view. If she recognised that other women behaved differently, she believed it was all right for them but not for her.

The script, though, is based on *old* decisions about yourself and your place in the world. It's information about the *past*: how you have been living *up to now*. That means you can start doing something different today to rewrite your personal film so you get a happier ending. But first it's helpful to see how those old, scripted ideas are lived out in the present. Could that help you identify problem beliefs so you know what you want to change?

How scripts are lived out
Now Heather had begun to recognise her Life Script, it was time for her to address the bits that were causing her problems.

There are six ways in which people live out their scripts. They are identifiable as repeating patterns of behaviours, which in turn are underlined by key words embedded in a person's beliefs about themselves. You may find that you have a combination of these script themes. Which ones do you recognise?

The process by which Heather had been living out her love life was an *always* script. Her refrain was, 'Why does this *always* happen to me?' From high-school dates through to her third husband, she'd *always* tried hard to please her man. Generally she stuck with him however unhappy she was because she believed that 'men are *always* like that' and that she'd *always* be powerless to do anything about it. When he was unkind, she might manipulate, nag or blow up at him if she felt safe. Then she'd try harder still to please him so she wouldn't end up alone. Though she couldn't really get close to her partner, from her powerless position she believed she was worthless without a man. An avid reader of problem pages, she'd discuss him endlessly with her female friends, asking their advice and then answering every suggestion with 'Yes, but I couldn't do that!' If you catch yourself asking for help and then saying, 'Yes, but . . . ,' could you have some *always* script?

With *always* scripts, as with the ones below, there are effective counters. Before we discover them, let's see how the other script processes might affect you.

Never

Ian was a solicitor, who was resentful that other people got promoted while he wasn't. Sometimes he'd moan about this to his few friends, but he *never* worked out effective strategies to gain promotion. His wife carped at him for his lack of drive so he avoided her when possible, or retreated into a daydream where he was a successful artist – though he *never* picked up a paintbrush or finished a drawing. He'd *never* wanted to be a solicitor but his parents told him he was just a foolish dreamer who'd have to buckle down in the real world because he'd *never* make it as an artist. *Never* scripts can leave you feeling stuck between alternatives.

Until

Robert obediently followed his father into the family business, feeling he couldn't have time for himself or his wife *until* he'd become successful. He believed working long hours earning money for his wife was the best way to show his love – but she felt neglected and had an affair. His answer was to work harder still so he could 'buy' her back with expensive holidays, but this expression of love couldn't happen *until* he'd earned enough. He had a heart attack.

Almost

Alison *almost* – but not quite – achieved her ambitions. She was shortlisted for a director's job but an outsider pipped her at the post. When she tackled a project, the first part would be brilliant but the end would be rushed and skimpy. She'd been engaged three times but had never married. **June**, on the other hand, had a different style of *almost* succeeding. She'd graduated from business school but carried on taking further qualifications while climbing the corporate ladder. Others envied her success but June couldn't be content because each time she *almost* achieved success, she'd set herself a harder goal. Like a mountaineer, she couldn't ignore the next peak she had to conquer.

After

Karl worked in PR. He arranged fabulous media events but couldn't enjoy them for fear something would go wrong. He wanted to work freelance but was afraid he'd fail if he tried. Whenever he finally got up the courage to ask someone for a date he'd stand them up because he was scared it would turn out badly. He believed that *after* he'd achieved an ambition, something terrible would follow.

Open-ended

All **Frances** had ever wanted was to be a wife and mother. But the children grew up and left home. Then her husband died. She'd lost what gave her a sense of identity and structure, meaning and purpose to her life. Now she was face to face with an echoing void.

Do any of these key-word themes ring bells with you? Do you, like Heather, want to free yourself and have more choices?

Rewriting your Life Script

So how do you edit your Life Script? Back to Heather.

In therapy Heather discovered that she'd been trying to make her life fit the ideas she'd accepted from her parents and the ones she'd developed for herself when she was little. In other words, she'd been living according to a script she herself had created. This gave her the power to start making changes. If you go back to the ideas Heather had generated about herself (*see page 21–22*), does that give you a starting point for the beliefs that have been causing you problems? How about writing those old beliefs down so you can start to update them? Here's how Heather began to reinterpret her rocky life with her husbands as meaning *these* men were neglectful, controlling or abusive.

- I'm unhappy when married to this sort of man.
- Some women prefer career, travel or female partners to heterosexual marriage.
- My friends' husbands Ted, Charlie and Allan are thoughtful and affectionate so men aren't always aggressive, etc., and wives don't always have to be subservient.
- Women married to nice men are happy. I wasn't happy because my husbands weren't nice to me. There's nothing wrong with me.
- Earning good money makes a good businessman, not necessarily a good husband.
- I lived on my own between husbands. I've often been happier alone or with my friends than with my husbands.
- Lots of proper women are divorced or unmarried.
- Mum moans a lot about Dad so her ideas don't make her happy either.
- Before we were married, I sometimes felt neglected or discounted but I ignored my feelings. Next time I'll act on them!
- My remarried exes are stuck in the same sorts of painful relationships so it wasn't all my fault.

If you too have felt trapped in a script that's heading for disaster, reality testing can help you overcome it. You can mentally give back those ideas to the people who generated them!

Challenging your key words

Heather now started to combat her key word of *always*. When she said to herself, 'Men are *always* this way and I'm *always* going to be helpless,' she felt unhappy and stuck. Instead she started to put limits on her *always* statements. 'My husbands were *often* aggressive or neglectful but *sometimes* they weren't.' 'I used to be passive but *from now on* I'll act assertively on my feelings.' '*Some* men are nice.' After all, if you keep doing the same things in the same ways, you're bound to keep getting the same results.

If you find the word *never* painful, try changing it to *sometimes, one day* or *a bit*. Then see if you feel any differently. Ian, the unhappy solicitor, started painting *a bit*. He joined an art class but his wife continued to nag – until he sold a painting. He realised he's the one who's living his life so he gets to say what he'll do with it. He's now divorced and happily living with a fellow artist in Majorca. His parents have had to let go of their old views of what Ian should be doing – but the free holidays help!

Robert, the workaholic, took his heart attack as a warning. In therapy he realised he wasn't valuable *only when* he'd completed a task but all the time as a human being, and as a husband who showed his love with attention and tenderness. He's learned to counteract his knee-jerk reaction to his *until* message with 'What do I want *now*?' Another inoculation against the perfectionism inherent in *until* is 'Good enough is good enough.' His wife rediscovered the man she'd loved and now they're generally happy together. She's been empowered by sharing some of his work.

The two forms of *almost* have separate counters. Alison learned to see a job through to the end, starting with little things like doing all the washing up and going on to complete each project carefully. She's been promoted. Now she's planning her time better, she's freed herself up to think more carefully about boyfriends before committing herself. June has started celebrating each of her achievements and using it to the full. More contented now, she's stopped chasing qualifications and begun to enjoy the lifestyle she's earned.

Karl challenged his *after* script by planning *now* to make *the future* as good as the present. He found a part-time contract to give him a regular income and began freelancing around it. He spends longer checking out potential partners and pacing his relationships so he won't get hurt.

Frances filled the void left by her *open-ended* script by shifting her focus from her lost goals of family life to find other pleasures like friends and interests.

What about you? Will you keep suffering the pain of being stuck in old themes or take up the challenge of editing your script?

A symbolic string to your bow

You could adopt another tactic that counters your beliefs on a symbolic level. This works because we don't respond directly to events but to what we think about them. A man who sees redundancy as failure will be depressed, but someone who thinks it's an opportunity to do something different will find it exciting.

What you do is find a story that reminds you of you, and then rewrite it. Heather related to Cinderella, who was bullied by her stepmother and sisters but was rescued by marrying a prince. Heather retold this story with Cinders no longer a helpless victim but a woman who recognised that she deserved a share of her father's estate. She took her fair share of the silver and left for the city. She still married the prince, but as she'd invested wisely she no longer felt dependent on him so they had an equal partnership.

In real life, Heather recognised her abilities and used them to make changes. She now feels good about herself and is optimistic about her future. She found a job, is training part-time to get a better one, and has joined a social club where she's made new friends. She hasn't found her prince yet but she's happy trying a few guys out for size. Will you rewrite your story?

One step at a time

Heather and the others didn't change overnight. Change can be scary so it's useful to make your changes small to start with. That way you can get used to them gradually. It helps if they're something you can measure. If your goal is to be happier, how will you know when you are? Asking yourself what you'll be *doing, thinking* and *feeling* helps you work out the steps you'll need to take. If necessary, break them down into even smaller steps. Then set yourself a realistic time limit for each one. You might like to give yourself a bit of leeway by setting *at least* goals. Ian's first one was to paint for *at least* two hours a week. Yours might be to work out which of your beliefs are worth keeping and which you want to change.

SUMMARY

Your adult life doesn't have to be an endless repetition of how things were when you were growing up. You can edit your script if you want to. It can be thrilling to take charge of your life, respecting yourself as much as you respect other people and knowing you're the only one who ultimately decides whether you're happy and successful on your own terms. You can adopt as much or as little as you're ready to, and you can get help if you ask. The longest journey starts with the first step. Are you willing to take it? I hope so!

Chapter 3

Throw Out Those Old Rules

Have you had a hard time making yourself heard? Now you can reshape the old beliefs that have been holding you back and learn to put your point across assertively.

Do people listen to you?

Kate and **Matt** seemed like any other couple when they came into the counselling room but one thing was obvious: Matt would look at his wife but she wouldn't meet his eye – or mine. It took some time for her to get up the courage to murmur, 'I know Mum's had a lot to put up with and she's only trying to help, but I'm fed up of her forever criticising the way I bring up my kids. It wouldn't be so bad if Matt would back me up but he doesn't. It's horrible when your mum has a go at you and your husband just agrees with her. The kids get away with murder and then you get all the blame. As soon as she's out of the door we have dreadful rows but he just walks away and nothing ever changes.' A lot of people don't feel heard. Instead they feel disregarded, discounted, invisible and impotent. If you've ever had that feeling you'll know how undermining it can be.

Even the shyest of people can learn to make themselves heard and valued. They can improve their relationships and find happiness as this couple have. I describe below how Kate learned to speak up for herself. Bear in mind that if Kate could do it, so can you! You'll find Matt's story later on but for now I'll concentrate on Kate's side of things.

Before she could comfortably use the assertiveness techniques you'll find later in this chapter, Kate needed to find and overcome the blocks in her thinking that had stopped her standing up for herself.

People like us

Any family has to have certain operating principles or it can't function. They help the members of the family know where they are in the scheme of things. Whether supportive or destructive, these principles form part of the architecture for the people living inside the family. Different families have different operating rules. For good or ill, they help make the members of a family *people like us*.

Generally these family rules won't be spoken aloud but I've put some of the ones I hear from clients into words. Depending on how they operated for you, you might want to put them in different categories. Which ones do you think Kate had taken in as a child? How were these beliefs preventing her from making herself heard? And what about you? I invite you to read them out loud one at a time. How do you feel about any that you recognise? Can you think of any others on which you've been operating?

Don't say what you feel because:

• Mum and Dad are always right. You're wrong to disagree.
• You can't discuss or acknowledge bodily functions.
• Nice people don't think about sex, talk about sex or have sex.
• Anger is wrong. It's dangerous, uncontrollable or just plain 'not nice'.
• You have to pretend you're happy and OK.
• Children aren't as important as adults. Their experience is inferior and invalid. This extends to you because you used to be a child.

There's something wrong with you:

• You're wrong to feel anything your parents don't want you to feel.
• You can't talk about [fill in your family's 'skeleton in the closet'], especially to outsiders.

- You can't ask outsiders for help with family problems. This is 'washing your dirty linen in public' and it's shameful.
- Outside authorities like teachers, the police, doctors and social services are out to get you.

How to belong:

- If you like different things you can't like each other.
- Your parents have the right to know every single thing about you but you can only know what they want you to know about them.
- Your parents can lie to you but you can't lie to them.
- If you don't spend all your free time in the same room as the rest of your family, you're disrespectful and there's something wrong with you.
- Women (or in some families men) aren't important.
- Saying 'I' is big-headed and selfish.
- If you don't know what I want without my asking, you don't love me.
- If you get what you want, you've won and I've lost.
- If you love me you'll do things my way.
- If you don't instantly know and understand, you're stupid.
- If you're not academically gifted (or sporty, musical, religious, artistic, good-looking, or financially like your family), there's something wrong with you.
- Fun is a sin or a waste of time.
- It's clever to lie, steal and harm outsiders so long as you don't get caught.
- It has to be our way. Change and difference are chaotic, dangerous, immoral or rude.
- Your place in the family, and therefore in the world, is fixed for all time.

Kate had accepted quite a few of these rules, hadn't she? You've probably realised that going along with them kept her believing she wasn't important in comparison with her husband and mother. She didn't believe she was good enough for either of them or for her kids. Kate actually dreaded her mother's visits to the point where she felt sick and shaky for hours beforehand, and was sometimes apprehensive before Matt came home from work.

Growing from an infant who wasn't allowed to ask for what she wanted, Kate also expected her husband to know what she needed without her saying. She was silently disappointed, swallowing down her anger 'like a good girl' when he didn't mind read her wishes and magically fulfil them. When she was disappointed enough she'd allow her anger to burst out in bitter recriminations. Because the ensuing rows were so hurtful, she maintained her belief that anger was inevitably dangerous – and, of course, she firmly believed her place at the bottom of the pecking order was fixed for the rest of her life.

What about you? What family rules have you now become aware of? How do you feel when you recognise them laid out in words? Would you change them if you could?

Is change allowable?

When Kate thought about her family rules she had an uncomfortable feeling in the pit of her stomach. It was compounded of anger and sadness. But she also felt apprehensive, as though even putting these beliefs into words would somehow bring retribution. (It didn't! Read on.)

As she bravely read the rules again, she realised with some indignation that other families had different rules, including ones that seemed to incite criminal behaviour. That was something her own family would never have contemplated. Those rules belonged not to *people like us* but to *people like them.*

So rules are not universally true! They're not necessarily good! Change and difference are possible!

Kate began to question whether her automatic beliefs had any real validity. Thinking back, she discovered that her family's rules had largely been for her parents' benefit rather than hers, at least in the short term. Instead of there being something intrinsically wrong with her that meant she couldn't make herself heard, she could now see there was something amiss with her view of her place as small and powerless in the world. And that could be updated. She could let go of the old rules.

To deal with her apprehension Kate decided to ask her friends for permission to make new, empowering rules like 'I can be important in my own life.' They gladly gave it.

Back at home Kate wrote out her list of old rules. Then she read them aloud one at a time, saying, 'This isn't mine and I don't want it any more,' and ceremonially tore them into little pieces, which she then binned. The next week she reported back how much better she felt. Making those beliefs concrete and destroying them is a powerful tool.

I invite you to consider how you felt about your family's rules when you were growing up. If you feel any sore spots, could updating your view of your place in the world help? Wouldn't it be great if you could speak up for yourself; if you could make yourself heard and valued? Because you can – as much as you're willing to. Here's the next step.

Passive, aggressive or assertive?

Taking in those old rules means that like Kate, a lot of people don't think they can personally ask for what they want with any chance of getting it. They therefore tend to show behaviours at opposite ends of a spectrum. Either they don't act to get what they want (sulking, martyrdom or pretending), which is passive, or they get to a pitch where they scream and shout, which is aggressive. Still more aggressive, of course, is emotional or physical bullying.

Passivity is frustrating. It sends the message that you feel like a helpless victim and regard other people as having all the power (I-U+). Aggression, oddly enough, also sends the message that the victim is the powerful one, because he has the power to grant the aggressor's wishes. Aggressive people come on as I+U-, but underlying that is a sadder I-U+. Aggressors try to control relationships by bullying, which ultimately alienates them.

Those old rules formed part of the architecture of your belief system. Now you're starting to get rid of them, what can you do instead? Comfortably in the middle of the passivity-aggression spectrum is assertiveness. Its central tenet is I+U+, that is, you respect yourself and the other person equally. You have the right to ask clearly and directly for what you want. The other person has the right to say no, but since you both know what you're talking about you can negotiate a compromise with no hard feelings on either side.

There are other advantages to you both knowing what you're talking about. You can stick to the subject until it's resolved or agree to disagree. There's no throwing in everything but the kitchen sink or raking up past hurts, so there's none of that hurtful battling to be top dog. Believe me, being assertive is the best way to avoid arguments! The joint decision-making process lines you up on the same side. Because you're both respecting your own feelings and each other's, you feel good about yourself and the other person even if you disagree.

Two other beliefs commonly leave people reluctant to say directly how they're feeling. The first is that emotions are either full on or full off. In fact, all emotions have degrees. You might be mildly annoyed, quite cross, angry or even lose your temper. These degrees are very different, but if you weren't allowed to be angry in your family home you wouldn't have had much chance to learn how to use anger safely. In that case you might have believed mild annoyance is the same as murderous rage. It's not! That belief was one reason Kate tried not to let anyone know when she was annoyed. She was afraid her anger would overwhelm her and she'd be powerless to stop it damaging herself and her family. She'd automatically believed that saying she was annoyed would mean her loved ones would reject her forever.

The other mistaken belief is that your emotions destroy other people, or take them over completely. That if you cry, your partner will be so sad he can't cope. That if you're cross, she'll either feel devastated or engulfed in a tidal wave of rage. That if you admit you're afraid, he'll dissolve into a terrified jelly – or mock you mercilessly.

But your emotions are yours, and how your partner responds is his choice. If he decides to weep, shake, stomp about, bully you or make fun of you for how you're feeling, that's not because of your emotion. It's what he chooses to do and you're not responsible for that. Believing your emotions have total power over others doesn't show much respect for them, does it?

Emotions make good servants but bad masters. They're a survival mechanism. From snakes to rabbits to cats and dogs, every animal needs emotion to survive and thrive. So do you. You're allowed to feel what you feel – and to act assertively on it, because if you don't value your feelings enough to act on them, why should anyone else?

Happiness tells you what you've got is good so keep doing it. Fear, anger and sadness tell you there's a problem so you need to do something to put it right. If you don't do anything, you might bury the feeling but it won't go away. It'll just lurk, biding its time, growing in the dark until it's so powerful that it bursts out.

In order to behave assertively, it's helpful to identify your feelings as soon as possible. For example, if you learn to recognise the symptoms that let you know you're starting to feel angry, you can ask for what you want before you go off pop. Or you could say, 'I'm starting to feel angry. I need a break to calm down. I'll be back in five minutes.'

Assertiveness techniques
What other assertiveness techniques did Kate begin to employ? Could you use them too?

Know what you want
Listening to your feelings helps you work out what you want. If you need to, why not break problems down into smaller, more manageable chunks? The problems won't seem so monolithic and overwhelming and it's easier to tackle things one bit at a time. What Kate wanted was better relationships with her children, her husband and her mother.

Say what you're feeling and what you want
Mind reading doesn't work. However much they love you, other people don't automatically know what you want. If you don't tell them, with the best will in the world they can still get it wrong. To start solving Kate's parenting problems, she decided to tell her husband, 'I feel helpless and unsupported when you leave the kids' behaviour management to me. Will you help me work out a policy we can both apply?' Matt was pleased but surprised. He'd thought (more mind reading) she'd be angry if he interfered. Now he too felt more valued and involved. This meant that the children could

no longer play one parent off against the other. As their behaviour improved, so did the atmosphere at home. That helpful formula goes, 'When you . . . I feel . . . so will you . . . instead?'

Make specific, brief requests

As Kate knew to her cost, rows, criticism and insults didn't force her husband to do things her way. Instead, he'd stomp off and leave her lonely and tearful. Piling one point on top of another only set his back up. Guilt trips alienated him. Antagonised, he'd fight back and the original point got lost in a power struggle. What did work was sticking to one idea at a time, preferably calmly, and using short, specific questions so that he could give his point of view as well. If there was a second problem, Kate could bring that up later once this one had been resolved.

Recognise what's going on for the other person

Making requests when the other person's stressed is counterproductive. Kate learned not to launch into a tirade about the children's naughtiness the minute her husband came home. After a hard day's work he needed time to unwind – and some nurturing. She started to sit down with him over cup of tea so each could listen to what was happening for the other and say what they wanted. She learned to say, 'You're looking tired. Are you?' In other words, she checked out his feelings, offering and inviting empathy.

Respect the other person's abilities and good will

When Kate yelled, 'You never help me!' she negated all the good things Matt was doing for his family. Unsurprisingly he was hurt and would insult her in return. Kate learned to show her appreciation of Matt's input and to ask for praise if she needed it. She let him know she was glad she could rely on him. Then both of them felt valued and supported.

ERO: Empathise, Reflect, Own

When Kate's hypercritical mother arrived to see the house Kate and Matt had moved into the day before, the mother said, 'It's very nice, dear, but it's an awful mess. The kids have left things all over the place. And when did you last wash up?'

In the past Kate would have taken on board her mother's condemnation so she'd have felt guilty, defensive and hostile. Now she *empathised*, that is, she acknowledged the emotion underlying her mother's viewpoint. She also *reflected* back what her mother meant, to make sure she'd understood. But then Kate *owned* her own feelings, thinking and behaviour. She said, 'You sound quite upset that we're still sorting things out. I'm a bit overwhelmed too. But we've done a lot and we'll soon get the rest cleared up.' The new, assertive Kate went on to say, 'I'd love a hand, though. Would you mind washing up while I make us a cup of tea?' Pleased to be of help, her mother now felt valued and involved.

Although Kate (and Matt) still had a long way to go, they felt they were at last travelling side by side along the road. As for how Kate continued to free herself from her mother's well-meaning tyranny, you'll find out in the next chapter.

SUMMARY

Family rules aren't always true for everyone. You can change them if you want to. The best way of making yourself heard is to speak up for yourself! Assertiveness is mutually respectful. By avoiding criticism and by making your requests directly, you increase your chances of getting what you want.

Chapter 4

Setting Safe Boundaries

If you've been bullied or put upon, wouldn't you like some ways to keep yourself safe? Here's how you could break out of that old victim mould and find positive ways forward.

I and You

In the last chapter you saw how Kate began to apply some assertive behaviours. Although she'd been thinking this would cause more friction, it actually minimised family tensions so everyone began to feel better. All the same, I invite you to read Kate's opening statement (*see page 28*) again because it illustrates some more important ways in which people can liberate themselves from the chains of the past.

Firstly, since Kate's goal was to make herself heard, don't you think it's significant that she began by giving her mother's point of view rather than her own? And secondly, on several occasions Kate used the words 'you' and 'your' when she was talking about herself.

People can run into problems when they have unclear boundaries around themselves. Like Kate, they may not trust their own experience and so become enmeshed in other people's judgements and desires. If you're not sure where your boundaries are, it's easy to take on other people's hurtful beliefs and even assume responsibility for other adults' feelings and actions.

If you've gone through this you'll know how painful it is. You'll recognise too that feeling of drifting helplessly through life, carried along like so much flotsam at everyone else's whim.

Building safe boundaries around yourself can help you know who you are. Instead of feeling at the mercy of everyone around you, you can begin to put yourself in the driving seat of your own life. Start by learning where other people end and you begin.

Why don't people have safe boundaries around themselves?

Most of my clients use 'you' a good part of the time when they mean 'I'. Try watching TV chat shows and see how many celebrities use 'you' to describe their own experience. Do you ever do this? I know I sometimes do! It's a typical speech pattern just about everyone has heard or used themselves – but sometimes, as with Kate, using it excessively indicates deep uncertainty about personal boundaries and causes all sorts of trouble.

The commonest positive intention of using this speech pattern is to appear modest – as someone who doesn't put themselves forward unbecomingly or come across as arrogant. (A lottery winner, for instance, might say, 'It's nice when you get a bit of good luck, isn't it?') It can be a cultural or family pattern, so using it may give a sense of belonging and identity. ('You know where you are when your mam's a Scouser.') Sometimes it's seen as friendly and warm. ('When you go down the club every week you're one of the gang, aren't you?')

Using this speech pattern can, however, have its downside too. Many people use 'you' when they mean 'I' to show that they are 'normal', often because they're scared they aren't, so it can be intended as a defence against the fear of rejection. I've heard battered women dismiss their injuries with, 'You get rows in every family, don't you?' With others, it's a sign that they don't trust their own perceptions or actions. ('Well, you have to button your lip when your boss is bullying you, don't you?') They try to identify what they're thinking and feeling with another person's viewpoint in order to give themselves some validity. As you saw in the last chapter, some people also believe that if they're different from others they won't be able to form attachments. ('You have to support your husband's football team, don't you?') Besides, you don't have to do anything different if you think your experience is the same as everyone else's.

In a small way this is what Kate was doing – but look how much trouble she'd created for herself! She felt vulnerable to everyone else's ideas, which swamped her own and left her feeling helpless. So why do people do this?

When we start out as babies, we can't care for ourselves; we can't move either away from danger or towards pleasure and safety. We need someone older to supply all the adult thinking and parent craft to ensure our well-being. I'm sure you've heard a mother say to her child, 'I'm cold. Put your coat on,' as though there's no boundary between her feelings and the child's. Helping a child learn to identify his feelings and act constructively on them is great – but only if the parents are then willing to let him grow up into an individual who may make different choices. That might not happen for various reasons. Here are a couple of the most common. Do you identify with any of them?

It can be hard to disentangle yourself from parents who are clingy or needy, or from those who are repressive. All that teenage rebellion is actually a way for a child to put clear, safe boundaries around himself so he can eventually head out on his own. But if the parental response is overwhelming the child may not complete his individuation because he doesn't feel safe to do so. In fact some parents are so invasive or have such weak boundaries themselves that the child never gets the chance to learn where he ends and other people begin.

It's when a child *doesn't* learn to be a separate individual that problems arise in adulthood. Either he'll grow up afraid to let anyone get close in case they take over his life completely, or he'll want to take *them* over completely because that's his understanding of love. In extreme cases you might find murderous jealousy or such dependence on a cruel partner that emotional illness, serious injury or death could result. If you find yourself confronting serious threats to your well-being, go and see your doctor and a psychotherapist. You are allowed to be safe and get help. There's a list of helpful resources at the back of this book. Here, though, I'm dealing with more everyday problems with separation and individuation. Let's see how it worked with Kate.

At work or with friends Kate had had no real difficulty, beyond perhaps a certain tendency to feel guilty, overworked, used and vulnerable to other people's moods ('You have to button your lip') but she generally functioned well. With people she loved such as her parents, husband, children and brother, it was different: she didn't know how to put in appropriate boundaries.

This meant feeling scared and powerless to manage her children's behaviour; seeing their naughtiness as signs that she was useless and they didn't love her; interpreting her husband's and mother's criticism in the same light; and absorbing their anger as a weapon she had to use against herself. When she told herself off, as she frequently did, she used phrases like, 'You're useless! You never get anything right!' This, of course, overshadowed her many good points and undermined her self-esteem, making her even more vulnerable.

She mistrusted her own judgement (even though she was the one living her life), and relied on the judgements of her parents or her husband. Even her brother's good-natured teasing was something she interpreted as a life-blocking put-down that meant she'd never be as important, successful or lovable as him. She mistakenly believed that sticking up for herself would mean her loved ones would cut off from her. Seeing herself as incomplete without all these people, she believed (although not consciously) that if they rejected her she would cease to exist.

Without a clearly defined boundary around herself, Kate expected her family to mind read her wishes while feeling a failure if she couldn't mind read – and fulfil – theirs. She was prey to, and responsible for, emotional blackmail such as guilt trips, shaming and blaming. She'd overburden herself by taking on other people's feelings and duties, and dreaded showing her emotions (except 'permitted' but false happiness), because she thought they'd overwhelm her family and she'd be left alone.

As you can see, it wasn't much fun being Kate. There may be parts of this that ring true for you as well. If so, you have my sincere sympathy because I know what it can be like. Are you willing to take permission to start doing something different: being your own, lovable, unique and valuable self?

Becoming 'I'

One of Kate's first tasks was simply to listen to herself speak. Each time she caught herself saying 'you' about herself, she was to replace it with 'I'. Matt wanted to help her, which was meant lovingly, but

Kate realised she had to start taking responsibility for herself. Although it's easy to talk about, changing that lifetime habit took a while. Unlike with some therapeutic techniques, there's no sudden, road-to-Damascus revelation with this one, just a gradual strengthening of self.

Learning to use 'I' and 'you' appropriately is one of the keystones in personal development and I can't emphasise enough the improvement in communication and self-esteem that it brings. I do hope you'll try it.

You saw in the last chapter how Kate also threw away some of the old operating rules she'd inherited from her family. She chose Matt as one of the people whose permission she sought so that she felt protected and safe making those decisions about what she'd believe from now on. It was her choice, though, whether she'd take those permissions in and use them. That helped her feel ready to take responsibility for getting her needs met. By telling Matt openly how she felt and what she wanted him to do, she helped the pair of them unblur their boundaries so there was much less blaming and far fewer guilt trips. A lot more work got done because they weren't wasting their time on quarrels.

Instead of guessing Matt's thoughts and feelings incorrectly from what he did or didn't do, she decided to ask him about anything that troubled her. Now she could say, 'When you read the paper at the dinner table, I feel devalued because you don't listen to me. Are you devaluing me?' Matt wasn't, but he now understood why she'd get ratty at mealtimes. He said he'd been shutting off out of pique because he sometimes felt she ignored him, preferring to pay attention to the kids. Now their feelings were out in the open they realised they'd been misinterpreting each other's actions. They decided that until the children could feed themselves reasonably well, the adults would snack during the children's mealtimes and eat together once the children were in bed. By owning and expressing their feelings they cut loose from self-criticism and built greater closeness.

You are not 'it'

Another way in which Kate had been maintaining her old power-less position was by externalising her feelings. You may remember her saying in her opening remarks, 'It's horrible' and 'Nothing ever changes'. By using those impersonal terms *it* and *nothing*, she had been expressing the view that those things were outside her and therefore beyond her control.

With Kate this wasn't too serious. It didn't take her long to realise that if she didn't do anything differently, nothing would change – but if she took action she could maximise her chances of getting a more positive outcome.

For some people, though, *it* can be life-threatening or at the very least emotionally crippling. I remember a client describing a self-defeating pattern of thoughts and behaviour as overpowering. What she said was, '*It* takes me over. I can't do anything about *it* because *it* controls my thinking.' *It* didn't. She came to realise that she was the one who chose to hang on to those thoughts and act on them. No one can stop what pops into their minds – but you can choose whether to pursue those negative thoughts or shift your focus to something positive. Once you realise that you are the one who gives negative thoughts houseroom they no longer have power over you. You start having power over them.

Other typical 'its' are anxiety and depression – but they don't exist outside yourself. No one is to blame if they begin to suffer from either of these. If, however, you realise that they're seldom caused by a situation, only generally by your response to a situation, you can begin to overcome them one step at a time.

Even if you're diagnosed with anxiety or depression, do remember that you're more than just a diagnosis. You're a worthwhile human being with many skills and good qualities. Whatever has happened to you, you deserve love, both your own and other people's. You can learn to think differently. Life is about change. If you're suffering from anxiety or depression you can get help – and you can start changing the way you think so you feel more relaxed and confident. There's more about overcoming anxiety and depression on my website at www.emotionalmagic.net but for now, back to Kate.

More boundary work

Now Kate had stopped externalising her feelings and started taking charge of her life, she was pleased at the positive changes with her husband and children. Far more scary, though, was the thought of disentangling herself from her mother. Because she'd been so in tune with her mother's way of operating, she was worried that her mother would find this a real threat and so would apply even more emotional pressure to pull the situation back to its old stability.

As you'll remember, the old operating principles had been unconsciously designed by Kate's mother and father in order to keep the family together and functioning on the parents' terms. Sure, the rules had ultimately been intended for the good of Kate and her brother – but the fallout from them was hindering Kate's happiness. She wasn't too sure how she'd react, either!

Kate challenged that old 'it' thinking by telling Matt, 'I feel horrible when you don't defend me against Mum's put-downs. Please will you stick up for me?' Matt wasn't too keen on the idea because he disliked confrontation, but he did agree he wouldn't join in when her mother criticised her.

Kate was now ready to tackle her mother's interference. An opportunity soon arose. Kate and Matt had laboured until almost midnight to finish fitting a new kitchen cupboard. It was dusty work. Proud but tired, they went to bed – and overslept. Next morning Kate's parents arrived half an hour early. Kate hadn't had a chance to do all her usual pre-mum cleaning up.

No sooner had Kate kissed her mother than that good lady ran a finger along the top of the coat rack, saying, 'This is filthy, Kate! And look at the state of your windows! They're covered in dust! I'd be ashamed to show my face if this was my house.' Kate could feel her face growing hot with anger. She found the remarks so hurtful that she was shaking. Her father, as usual, avoided the row by going for a walk in the garden.

Kate shot Matt a pleading look and he rose to the occasion. He gave Kate a chance to calm down by taking over the welcoming while Kate made a cup of tea. Then Kate sat down and said, 'Mum, I love you and I'm really grateful for all your help, but when you criticise me I feel hurt and angry and I want to cut off from you. I don't want that. Do you?'

Her mother blustered, 'Well, if I'm not wanted I'll go right back home. I'll never see you again, then you'll be happy!'

Kate said, 'I'd hate that, Mum. I love you, but I don't like you criticising me.'

Crying with humiliation and rage, the mother replied, 'You should be ashamed talking to your mother like that!'

Kate, though still trembling, said quietly, 'I hate it when you yell at me. You're lovely most of the time but do you want to be known as the woman who yells?'

The mother said blamefully, 'Well if you'd only do things right in the first place I wouldn't have to yell.'

Kate replied, 'I'm sorry you don't like the way I do some things but I'd like you to acknowledge I do some things well too, then we could feel closer to each other. Wouldn't you like that?'

Eventually, both weeping, they fell into each other's arms for mutual comfort. Although Kate's mother never referred to this conversation again, she's now giving less criticism and more praise. Things are still far from perfect between them, but now Kate quite looks forward to short visits. She's also planning on asking her father for his support. And since she's asked Matt for his help and protection, life is better all around for Kate and her family.

SUMMARY

Separating yourself from your family is liberating. It doesn't have to mean cutting off from them – although some people make an adult decision to do so in order to stop themselves from being engulfed by invasive family members. What it does mean is not automatically taking on other people's thoughts, feelings or behaviours, but using your own to keep yourself safe. It's also important to remember that you are not your actions. We all make mistakes – but we do lots of other things too, most of which are neutral and some of which are good. You can take power over what's happening to you by remembering that you are not 'it' but a worthwhile human being on your journey through life.

Chapter 5

Building New Bonds with Your Siblings

Sibling squabbles can cut deep. If you want to resolve problems between yourself and your brothers or sisters, here are some effective techniques for revitalising the bonds between you.

The unthroned princess

'What a clever girl you are to give me such a lovely grandson!'

Greta felt she'd waited all her life for this praise from her mother. She was moved to tears because finally she felt valued. She even dared to hope that her mother, **Mrs A**, would stop beating her up emotionally for not being a rich high-flier like her perfect sister **Rowena.** The doting grandma bullied Rowena into visiting the new wonder-child. She hardly noticed the swanky Porsche in which Rowena took her on the pilgrimage. When they got to Greta's run-down flat, Mrs A interrupted Rowena's story of her glamorous holiday in the Bahamas with cooings and baby worship.

Rowena was hurt. Over the crib she told her sister, 'You want to lose weight. That top does nothing for you.' Greta snapped back, 'What would you know about anything? You're just a yuppie stick insect with an empty life.'

Rowena felt like a princess who'd been pushed off her throne. As she drove her mother away, she made sly digs about how irresponsible her sister was to have a child she couldn't afford. She capped it off by saying, 'Well I'm not lending her any more money!'

Rowena's letting the cat out of the bag about her loans gave Mrs A new weapons to attack Greta.

Do you too have a prickly relationship with your siblings? Have you been sad that one of the longest relationships you'll ever have in your life is difficult or cold? Does it hurt you that someone with whom you've shared so much doesn't seem to like you? If you do, then maybe, like Greta and Rowena, you'd like to update your view of yourself, your siblings and your place in the world. By changing an emotional minefield into a warm alliance, these sisters also found new confidence in themselves.

Who's at the centre of your stage?

The first step is to find out where these prickles come from. It's always easier to see these things from the outside, so here's how it worked for Greta and Rowena.

Mrs A had managed well with her first-born, but when Greta came along a couple of years later, Mrs A didn't have the energy to cope with another child too. From babyhood, Greta's task was to try and break into the pre-existing mother-daughter bond. Rowena didn't want to be deprived of that life-giving closeness and did her best to keep her little sister out of it by being as perfect as she could. That was her task. The sisters jockeyed for position, overtly by putting each other down and covertly by telling tales and showing off.

As she grew up Greta often saw herself not from her own perspective, but as a kind of disregarded extra in a play where Rowena hogged all the limelight. Believing she was stupid, ugly and worthless because she wasn't like her perfect elder sister, Greta adopted a *never* script. This meant she was unlikely to acknowledge her feelings or act on them and so tended to give up. She thought that as she could never earn her mother's approval, she'd never win anyone else's. Even when she left home she kept acting out her *never* script by drifting in and out of unfulfilling jobs and relationships. She came to therapy when her partner literally left her holding the baby, never dreaming that one day she'd end up with Rowena as her closest friend.

As an adult, Rowena continued to be the golden girl. Her need to get the better of others was based on her jealousy of the younger sister who came along and 'stole' the attention that 'should' have been hers. At work she swam through a competitive industry like a shark, associating with people who were also scrambling over each other on their way up the corporate ladder. Unconsciously believing that only her accomplishments gave her worth, Rowena hid her essential loneliness under her triumphs. She lived by the unacknowledged belief that she couldn't rest until she'd done everything perfectly. You'll realise this is part of the *until* script, though there are elements of *almost* too.

The feelings the girls experienced were too complex for them to resolve when young and too painful to carry consciously, so neither of them had ever questioned their belief that the other girl was just naturally unpleasant. They didn't see that they themselves could behave differently. Mrs A kept the system going by sighing over the way 'poor' Greta could never do as well as the perfect Rowena. Neither sister stopped to think how their attitudes to this parental input warped their relationship with each other.

Why not ask yourself who's at the centre of your internal stage? What effect might your response to parental input have on your relationship with your siblings?

Parental input

Perhaps you can relate to how the Greta-Rowena system led each sister to believe that the other – and, indeed, she herself – was essentially unlovable. They had believed their relationship was a simple one:

Greta ———————— Rowena

In fact, the relationship had been deformed by the mother's input, so that it was more like:

Mrs A wasn't evil. She loved both her girls and wanted them to be happy. She believed Rowena's behaviour was the best recipe for happiness and so wanted Greta to behave in a similar fashion. Parents don't have to do anything wrong. Their mere presence affects how children see their siblings.

Even if the parents were perfect there'd still be some of that warping. We don't grow up in a vacuum. Each significant person acts like a centre of gravity so that brothers, sisters, parents, grandparents and so on all exert a pull on relationships. For example, Greta and Rowena's view of each of their parents was affected by the other parent's presence too.

This deformation may be particularly virulent with twins, as in the case of **David** who was delicate and **Jonathan** who was sturdy. Their mother, who was not the healthiest person emotionally, blamed healthy Jonathan for 'stealing' his twin's nourishment in the womb. She was angry when Jonathan's boisterous demands interrupted her caring for his brother. Until the age of eight, the boys would have said they hated each other. Certainly they fought a lot, often at the secret instigation of delicate David who could then coax treats from his mother by saying his stronger twin was bullying him. It was only when they went to boarding school that David found out what real bullying was. Powerless as older boys stuffed his head down a flushing toilet, David was saved by his brother. After that the twins formed a warmer partnership.

In both these cases you're seeing sibling rivalry in operation, in a system involving the mother as well as her offspring. I agree that children, with their limited thinking and somewhat egocentric world-view, can be spiteful and possessive, fighting over trifles and taking umbrage over imagined slights, but generally these contretemps leave less scarring than that earliest of wounds, the primal struggle to find your own place in your family. Here are some other ways in which parental input can deform brother-sister relationships. Do any of them feel familiar to you?

Enmeshing

Liz idolised her protective older brother **Geoff** and was hurt when he left to live in Australia, scarcely ever making contact. She had no idea what she might have done to upset him. Feeling abandoned, Liz was hostile when Geoff rang so he was cold in return. In therapy she realised that he'd fled from his mother and father to avoid being drawn into inappropriate parental responsibilities. Once she knew that his reasons for leaving had nothing to do with her, Liz recovered fond memories of their shared childhood games. She responded warmly when he rang again and was delighted when he invited her to visit him.

Gender prejudice

This is another powerful deformation. Some parents value one gender over the other. The dominant gender may lord it over siblings of the subordinate gender, who often feel deeply unlovable. Any gender-prejudicial set-up can result not just in painful sibling rivalry, but also in neglect, abuse and despair.

Parental exhaustion

This can happen if parents are overburdened, growing old or have many children. Some children then feel neglected because their parents don't have the strength to take care of them. As a consequence they may feel worthless, sometimes with corresponding poor treatment from their elder brothers and sisters. Alternatively, they may become difficult in order to force their demands for attention on their parents. Such insecure behaviour can carry over into adulthood, sometimes in frightening anti-social ways as adult powers are gained.

'Parentification'

This is what occurs when an elder child is required to look after younger ones, or any child is required to take care of his parents. The child taking on this parental role can develop a lifelong pattern of looking after others' needs at the expense of his own.

'Infantilisation'

This is something that happens when parents have damaging concepts of ageing and losing their value and so try to keep one child tied to their apron strings. Someone who's been infantilised may still be living at home in their forties, wanting to be an adult but constantly being treated as a child. Siblings may belittle the infantilised child while being jealous of 'Mummy's favourite'.

Perceived parental tyranny

This is a by-product of strict parenting. The parents probably believe they are acting in the children's best interests though the children themselves feel repressed. Children may form a strong us-versus-them alliance against parents they perceive as tyrannical. This allows some sense of belonging despite any sibling rivalry.

Family slots

These can have painful effects. We've seen how Rowena and David were each considered the 'Golden Child' who could do no wrong, while Greta and Jonathan were the 'Scapegoat'. There are other potentially damaging family slots, as you'll see in the next chapter.

Parental input isn't necessarily bad. Most parents aren't actually cruel or overbearing. Childhood thinking is underdeveloped and children don't see consequences as adults do, so that setting safe limits for children can seem like repression. Perhaps as a teenager you hated having a curfew but your parents imposed it because they didn't want you to be mugged or raped. Children don't always have the chance to make comparisons with what's happening in other families so they may form an unbalanced perspective. Even the most wonderful parents sometimes do and say things that the immature child finds hurtful.

Being aware that your parents aren't perfect isn't disloyal. The message received isn't always the one that's sent. You've already learned in earlier chapters how to disentangle parental messages to find the good things about yourself. Now you can do the same thing with your brothers and sisters. This can allow you to forge a much more rewarding relationship with them.

Building new bonds

To do this you can start by finding the answers to some questions about your siblings. The idea is to update your view of that person *without* the deforming parental aspect you learned as a child. Don't forget that deformation can occur simply by the parent(s) existing and not because he or she did anything wrong. It's about your decisions, remember? You can work through all the questions for each member of your generation with whom you've had problems. As the first parts of this exercise can bring up painful childhood feelings, why not have a comforting drink to hand, and organise a treat afterwards to reward yourself for your bravery? Best of all, you can look forward to the uplifting liberation from those old ideas.

I invite you to read through the whole exercise first. It starts with you updating your view of your sibling, and continues with you providing your view of how you've been comparing yourself to the sibling. So you can see how the exercise works, I've given the questions with Greta's answers. Afterwards you'll find the questions repeated so that you can fill in your own answers.

Greta's appraisal of her sibling:

Is your sibling happy?

> No, Rowena's a lonely, miserable workaholic who has to boast and put others down to feel OK about herself.

Does she still feel obliged to fulfil the role into which your parents invited her?

> Yes, hence the workaholism and her expensive keeping-up-with-the-Joneses lifestyle.

Does this cost her time and energy? What else does it cost her?

> Rowena's constantly tired and stressed. Her friendships are shallow and competitive, built around social climbing rather than caring. Her partner is equally ambitious so he's often out and she misses him, or she's stuck preparing elaborate dinner parties to impress his bosses. She's scared he'll trade her in for a better model so she's always on a diet or at the gym.

How does she value her own feelings in comparison with your parents'?

> She's making herself ill in her quest to carry on being their golden girl. Her triumphs don't fulfil her so she forces herself to work harder still. Her life isn't her own. Her feelings about herself are too dependent on Mum and Dad's stingy praise.

Can you remember times when she was angry with your parents?

> Yes. She worked ridiculous hours all through school and college and really resented them pushing her – particularly as they'd given up on me so I didn't get the same pressure. But she never dared stand up to them.

I hope Greta's appraisal of Rowena has let you see how even the golden child has feet of clay. Once you stop measuring success or failure in your parents' terms and start looking at your sibling as an individual, it helps you take the gilt – or the mud – off her.

The second phase of building new bonds relates to how you see yourself in comparison with your siblings. Again, why not read on to see how Greta worked this before you answer in relation to your own brothers and sisters?

Greta's appraisal of herself in comparison to her sister:
What decisions about yourself did you make in relation to your sibling?
Compared to Rowena I thought I was lazy, stupid, ugly, unimportant and unlovable.
Did she wind you up or purposely make trouble for you?
She made trouble for me by being 'perfect' in a grovelling kind of way and by telling tales to Mum. Sometimes she was snappy and put me down.
Why do you now think this was?
She was permanently stressed, as well as jealous if I got any positive attention.
Do you think she was happy with how your parents treated her?
No, or she wouldn't have felt pressured or needed to be jealous.
What does that mean about you?
She obviously thought I had some power. I must have enough good points to be a strong rival.
What can you now decide about yourself?
I'm glad I'm not Rowena. I feel sorry for her. I don't want to be like her. I have my own good qualities and I can value them even if my family don't. Mum and Rowena aren't happy so why should I follow their views? I'll be successful my own way.
Do you have any good memories of your sibling?
She helped me when I was stuck with my homework. Sometimes she played with me. She gives me nice presents. After Dave left she lent me some money. She was good company on family holidays.
What do you want to do differently about your sibling?
She's insecure so instead of making digs I'll ignore her boasting and bolster her. I'll spend time with her while her partner's away.

The Results

Greta stopped holding on to her view of herself as a minor character in a play where her sister had centre stage. As she said, 'This is my life. I want to be the star of my own play.' Greta now began to put more energy into becoming the person she wanted to be. She signed up for a government-sponsored course at a college with a creche, and joined Gingerbread, an organisation offering support and companionship for single parents (*see* Resources, *page 206*). She also rang Rowena, catching her crying because she was worried about her husband's fidelity.

The two women came to form a mutually supportive alliance and even started laughing about the three-handed game of 'good daughter, bad daughter' they'd been playing with their mother. In a later conversation Rowena told her sister how envious she'd been of Greta's talent for friendship and fun while Rowena was plugging away at her studies.

Building your own new bonds

Here are those questions again to enable you to update your view of your siblings and yourself.

Appraising your sibling:

- Is your sibling happy?
- Does she still feel obliged to fulfil the role into which your parents invited her?
- Does this cost her time and energy? What else does it cost her?
- How does she value her own feelings in comparison with your parents'?
- Can you remember times when she was angry with or resentful of your parents?

Appraising yourself:

- What decisions about yourself did you make in relation to your sibling?
- Did she wind you up or purposely make trouble for you?
- Why do you now think this was?
- Do you think she was happy with how your parents treated her?
- What does that mean about you?

- What can you now decide about yourself?
- Do you have any good memories of your sibling?
- What do you want to do differently about your sibling?

SUMMARY

The way you compare yourself to your siblings isn't always based on realistic perceptions. By filtering out parental input and childhood decisions, you can update your view of yourself and your siblings so that you make new, supportive decisions about yourself and your future relationship to each other and the world. This means you have the choice whether or not to be close.

Chapter 6

Building Your New Role

Has your role in the family caused you problems? Here's how you can start breaking out of the mould and find positive ways forward.

What was your function in your family?

Strange as it may seem, each of the children in a family has a separate function – and let's not forget that parents have functions too! Some of these can be rewarding. If you're the musical one, you can get praise and attention for a skill that gives pleasure to yourself and other people. If you're the boisterous one you're probably good at making friends and having a laugh, while if you're the quiet one you may enjoy your solitary pursuits. Not all functions are positive, however, at least for those fulfilling them. Some are downright dangerous. If you're wondering what functions there are, and whether yours could be causing you problems, read on.

Daddy Bernadette

Bernadette finally pushed herself into therapy because she was terrified she was going mad. She suffered panic attacks and often felt as though she was not present in her own body. She wasn't sure what she wanted out of therapy beyond 'not feeling like this any more'. Her dream of getting married didn't figure as a goal in Bernie's thinking because she didn't believe it was possible.

Together we explored Bernie's life. The youngest child, she was now in her thirties. She was the only one in her family working full-time. Her father, **Mick**, formerly a beefy construction worker, was now retired. After decades of alcohol abuse he'd dwindled into a shadow and wanted constant attention. Her brother **Liam** suffered from chronic fatigue syndrome. If she went out she was supposed to take him with her. Meanwhile mother **Noreen** was a school cook with a part-time waitressing job, which meant she had little time to look after her invalids.

After her day's work Bernie had to entertain her housebound brother and do all the heavy housework because her mother had sciatica. She had to hand over a hefty portion of her meagre wage and help her mother sort out the paperwork and bills. On her father's bad days she had to help him up to bed. She had to sympathise with her mother's burdens since Noreen wouldn't talk intimately to anyone else (that old 'washing dirty linen in public' myth). In other words, Bernie had to be the daddy. But if that was her role, what were the roles of the rest of her family? What is your role in your family? Do you relate to any of the 'family slots' – the categories described below?

The Caretaker

Bernie's job in life was taking care of everyone else so the family could stay together and still function. She was enmeshed in inappropriate parental responsibilities – emotional as well as practical ones – with the result that she had no energy or time to live her own life. Noreen believed she herself was the Caretaker. Are you yourself in any way a caretaker in your family? If you are, how do you feel about it?

The Golden Child

Rowena from the last chapter had to excel in order to win positive attention from – and for – her family. While this brought material success it didn't bring her happiness. In Bernie's family the Golden Child slot was occupied by the memory of the oldest child who had died in infancy. It can be hard fighting the power of a 'ghost'! If you're the Golden Child, are you happy about it? And how do your brothers and sisters feel about you?

The Scapegoat

This is the one who gets blamed for everything. Rowena's sister Greta was the family Scapegoat. Her job in life was to carry all the family's negative feelings so they didn't have to. They could also feel good about themselves because they were one up on her. The Scapegoat continually feels she's a disappointment. This can be particularly painful if the Scapegoat is one of twins where the other is the Golden Child.

The Rebel

The Rebel may or may not occupy the same family slot as the Scapegoat. Rebels might become the 'black sheep of the family', the one they don't talk about. Sometimes a Rebel cuts off from, or is exiled by, the rest of the family. Her function is to show the rest of the family that they've got it right. Rebels often have mixed feelings about themselves.

The Pathetic One

Some people don't know how to stay in contact with their family except by being ill. You may have relatives of your own who enjoy ill-health and use it as a weapon for emotional blackmail. Illness doesn't have to be part of a family slot. It may be just a random result of accidents or bugs.

The source of pity doesn't have to be physical ill-health. It could be any other area where the Pathetic One is seen as a failure by her family. The Pathetic One's task is to keep the family together to care for her. In Bernie's family three people were competing for this slot: both parents and the surviving son.

The Identified Patient

Being in this slot is very similar to being the Pathetic One. The difference as I see it is that the Identified Patient is more likely to suffer from emotional difficulties than physical ones because her job in life is to carry the family's conflicting emotions. By piling them onto her, they don't have to deal directly with the conflicts. Then they can blame her for not getting things right. 'After all,' they tell each other, 'she's the one who's the doctor's patient.'

The Triangulated Child

Parents who don't get along well may each feel the need to have someone on their side. If they invite their child into that supporting role, his loyalties become torn, particularly if the parents demonise each other. Rather than feeling that he has a clear, one-to-one relationship with each of his parents, he may feel that he's always the third point of a triangle. This triangulation leaves him uncertain of who he is and what intrinsic value he has, since he needs to behave differently with each parent for them to feel better about themselves. He usually worries about what he'll be like when he grows up since he was born from demonised parents. If this has happened to you, do you want to recover from it?

The Pawn

Sometimes triangulation is extended so that 'possession' of the child becomes a weapon in the parents' battle. A divorced father may decide that as his wife doesn't love him any more he'll hurt her by ignoring the child. A divorced wife might refuse the father parental access out of spite. These actions are usually taken without considering the child's wishes, the excuse being that not having contact with the 'bad' parent will be best for her. In fact she's likely to feel that at least one of her parents doesn't love her and therefore she is (at least in part) unlovable. As a result of this, serious trust issues can arise in later life.

The Glue

Another slot doled out by parents in conflict can be the Glue that holds them together. Being responsible for holding warring adults together is a terrible responsibility for a child, and one where she's unlikely to feel like a winner since this task isn't within her power. As her parents are still together because of her, she's likely to feel guilty for 'causing' all the misery that goes on in the house. If ever you hear someone say, 'We're only staying together for the sake of the children', isn't it the children you feel sorry for?

The Mistake

Some conceptions aren't planned or desired. I've known of parents who've actually told their child they'd tried to abort him. He'll probably have little belief in his right to exist as himself and be lovable. Parents may do this as an excuse for their own inadequate resources or parenting skills. People who are given this slot may find it blends with another role like the Scapegoat.

The Puppet

Parents who haven't achieved their life-dreams may want a child who will grow up to do all the wonderful things that Mummy and Daddy couldn't. They use the child as a Puppet, disregarding her wishes and pushing her into achievements she doesn't really want. Parents may also intend the child to be an extension of themselves, for example a carbon copy who will take over the family firm and run it just like Dad does. Or children may be seen as accessories to be dressed like dolls. When they become teenagers with minds and fashions of their own they may no longer be wanted.

The Special One

All of these roles can be viewed as special – but special can have good connotations as well as bad ones. In some families, especially large ones, a child may need to develop some special skill to compete for positive attention from her family. Pleasant Special slots could be the Cute One, the Smart One, the Sporty One and so forth, and these can also combine with other slots. Imagine being fifty, though, and still trying to be the Cute One!

More unsettlingly, the Special One may be the one who is abused sexually, physically or emotionally. She may submit to this in order to protect younger siblings from the same abuse, to save her mother from the father's unwelcome attentions or simply because it's the only way of life she knows. Sadly, it may also be the only time she receives attention at home. She may be handed the blame for the abuser's behaviour. Abuse almost always occurs in an atmosphere of secrecy, so add that to her feelings of guilt and you can see why she may not feel she can ask for help. If this has happened to you, you're *not* responsible for the abuser's actions or feelings and I honour you for surviving. You can be safe and you can get help to rebuild your life. Some starting points are offered in the Resources section (*see page 202*).

It's worth realising that family slots don't necessarily cover every aspect of your life. Nor do they have to last a lifetime. Whatever family slot you may have had, don't forget that it's part of your *past* so you can do something different *in the present* to improve your *future*. For now, let's get back to Daddy Bernadette and see how she transformed her life. Could there be useful pointers here for you?

Breaking out of the mould

Before Bernie could move on psychologically, she needed to get over the panic attacks that were limiting her choices. She found it reassuring to know they weren't heart attacks, which have different symptoms.

One of the quickest counters to panic attacks is triangle breathing. You breathe in normally for a count of three, breathe out normally for a count of three and hold your lungs empty for a count of three. This tells your body it doesn't need a high level of anxiety hormones. You could also run your hand under the cold tap or make a cup of tea to help you shift your focus away from your panic and back to the external world. Medication can be a useful temporary tool to help you get past panic attacks.

Once Bernie realised that her panic attacks were her body's response to her internal conflict between wanting a life of her own and feeling that she ought to stay enmeshed in her family's system for their sakes, she experienced both terror and anger. She also began to wonder whether her symptoms were a subconscious play for the Pathetic One slot which so effectively won attention in her family.

Her first impulse was to rush back home and yell at everyone that they had to be different. But they didn't want to be different. What they were doing was working for them. Besides, Bernie recognised that she wasn't responsible for their thinking, feelings or actions, just for her own. She realised too that they would fight against her, a valuable part of the system, making any changes. She faced a tough choice: accept her family system as a part of herself forever, or separate out from them, preferably while not losing contact.

Struggling with indecision, Bernie experienced more panic attacks. Working out that now Liam was an invalid he'd stopped being invited into the Caretaker/Daddy slot, she wondered whether an emotional component aggravated the physical one.

She took this as a warning and resolved to make the changes she needed.

Her first task was to start *thinking* about how the family system worked and how she could safely step outside it. Recognising parallels between the family system and the dogsbody role she'd fallen into at work, she began to put limits on her responsibilities at the office and started rejecting the feelings her colleagues projected onto her: blame, panic and guilt if she didn't tidy up their loose ends. Buoyed by her small successes at work, she gradually started to apply the same principles at home.

She stopped waiting on her father and brother hand and foot, reminding them that doing things for themselves would help them build up their strength. This matched what the doctor said, so though her family were displeased, they couldn't complain too much.

Bernie also established a little corner of her own in her bedroom. She bought herself a TV and a bookstand. With a picture or two and some bright cushions she made it her retreat. By consciously devoting part of the evening to showing her family positive attention she won space from them. The family didn't like her cutting off from them, but she was relieved to spend time away from the stew of their emotions. She was beginning to use the way the system worked to make her escape.

Next Bernie set up a bank account for her mother with standing orders for the bills. She explained how the home finances worked to both Noreen and Liam, and made it clear that from now on she was going to leave them in charge of these matters. Her mother, who had never been good with money, had one or two disasters but soon learned how to deal with the finances when Bernie wouldn't put in extra to tide her over.

Then Bernie encouraged Liam and her father to go to night school. Mick took up pottery and Liam, poetry. They loved it! Although Bernie drove them there and back for the first couple of weeks, she then went to salsa lessons on the same night so her father started taking them in his car. Since it became apparent that he could drive when he wanted to, Bernie stopped doing the supermarket run. It meant some rows, but she'd survived rows before.

What Bernie had done was show her family that they could find ways of improving their own lives if she wasn't there to bail them out. After that she left them to it.

Finding new support for yourself

Now Bernie wasn't so enmeshed in her family, she had time and energy to invest in her own life. She made friends at her dance class, including men. Though it took time to screw up her courage, she began dating. This was something she hadn't done for years because in her experience men were aggressive, like her father when she was young, or demanding like her sickly brother. Now, though, she realised she had choices. She wasn't inadequate or responsible if they behaved badly, and she could walk away if she wasn't happy with them. She's still practising being herself with boyfriends, but her dream of marriage is now on the cards.

Bernie has also discovered that it's OK to ask for information you need. No one is born knowing how to get a mortgage. In the meantime she's looking for a flat share a mile or two from home. She's taking part-time vocational classes and has already found a better paid job with more status.

Bernie now feels she's fully present in her life. Her panic attacks are gone so she's enjoyed weekends away with friends. Her family are managing more without her. She's used to them saying she's selfish, but now knows that it doesn't mean she is!

SUMMARY

You are a separate person. You're responsible for your own feelings, thoughts and actions. Other people are responsible from theirs. It's your life to live so you can make self-supportive choices from now on. After all, your choices make a big impact on who you become. You can be kind and considerate, but you don't have to be a slave. You're lovable and valuable for who you are, not just for what you do. Just because you've been doing something a certain way up to now it doesn't mean you're obliged to continue doing so. You can make small, manageable changes that help you get closer to your goals.

Chapter 7

Family and Self-esteem

Could you have 'inherited' self-doubts from the people you grew up with? Here are some ideas for realising your own worth and building self-esteem.

Would you like more confidence?

Just about every person I've ever met sometimes has problems with self-esteem. Many high achievers are fuelled by personal insecurities. Steeplejacks can suffer agonies because they're scared around people. About one in three participants on my confidence courses are great at assertive complaints in shops but shrink from the mildest confrontation with family members. You may be brilliant at all sorts of things but at least some of the time – say, for instance, with stroppy teenagers or unfamiliar situations – are you plagued by self-doubt? It's only human – but are you happy about it? Wouldn't you like to be more confident if you could be?

What do you get from self-doubt?

When I ask people what they get from doubting themselves, they generally say 'limitations and misery'. So why do humans carry on doing something that seems to have only a downside? In actual fact, underneath that is a positive intention that's got lost along the way.

Take shyness. Shy people often feel desperately lonely. They'd be delighted not to feel isolated or used by their family. They'd love to have good relationships. But they believe they're powerless to do anything about it. That's the downside – at least on the face of it. So why would anybody do that to themselves?

If you don't make the first move, if you avoid eye contact and don't stand up for yourself, your motivation is probably to avoid criticism and rejection. But self-doubt gets you lots of time on your own, time when you can dwell on what you see as your weaknesses and give yourself a mighty telling-off. Far from shy behaviours helping you avoid criticism and rejection, that's exactly what you get from the expert on what hurts you: yourself.

The truth is that *you get what you're focused on.* If you focus on criticism, criticism is what you'll have in abundance. If you think you're unlovable, you're missing the one person's love that you need most: your own.

How did that work for **Jackie**? A kind, pretty woman in her thirties, she'd always believed she was naturally shy. Her nickname was 'Cat' since her stepbrothers tormented her by chanting their mother's mantra: 'Cat got your tongue?' She hid away so as not to attract their unwelcome attentions. Her own father was dead and her stepfather was the kind of man's man who was awkward and gruff around her so she kept away from him. A scared and lonely child, she'd done her best to avoid her mother's sarcastic criticism too.

At school and work Jackie had adopted the same tactics: head down, don't meet anyone's eye, keep quiet. Although she'd hoped to make friends, she'd unwittingly behaved in ways that walled everyone out. She came to therapy after a string of hurtful romances had left her friendless and forlorn. What she wanted most was a partner who'd always be there for her. The trouble was, her desperation resulted in her going out with anyone who asked and then clinging on for grim death however painful she found the relationship. Focusing on the loneliness she'd known since childhood, what she got was more loneliness.

Today Jackie is happy with a man who loves her and shows it. Where she used to hide her feelings, she's become vivacious. She now has lots of friends, generally good relationships with her colleagues and she's been promoted. So how did Jackie get from A to B? How did she manage to change self-doubt into confidence – and could you do the same?

Are you sabotaging yourself?

People almost always do their best. When it doesn't work they generally do the same things again, only more so, because it's the best or only plan they can think of. Often they become increasingly self-critical as they keep finding themselves back at square one. But if what you've done hasn't been working, why not give something different a go? Jackie wasn't convinced about this. She told me tearfully (and a bit resentfully), 'But I have been doing different things! I've gone to dances and night school but I'm still lonely.'

It was great that Jackie had widened her opportunities. However, wherever she went, she kept repeating the same isolating childhood tactics once she got there. This happened because underlying any of our behaviour is a belief system. It affects not only what we do but also what we think and how we feel. It probably seems true and inevitable because it's been there as long as we can remember.

Jackie had taken on board her mother's label: 'Cat got your tongue', deciding that speaking up for herself only invited trouble. She believed she was powerless and that as males had always been hurtful or had left her, there had to be something wrong with her. It had never even occurred to her that not all men behaved as her stepfather, brothers and her lovers so far had done, or that she could behave differently now she was an adult in the outside world. Once Jackie discovered she could update her old childhood patterns her life took a turn for the better.

There is such a thing as random fate. Maybe a train is delayed and you miss a wonderful opportunity through no fault of your own. Jackie's old response to bad luck was, 'Typical! That always happens to me. I'll never get what I want.' But as she became more confident she realised she could make her own opportunities. How did she start doing things differently? Are you willing to do the same?

Write down your old beliefs

Your first step towards changing the way you've been thinking is to identify your old beliefs so you know what you're going to update. List them as suggested below, then write down your responses to them. Writing down your old beliefs can provoke lots of bad feelings you remember from childhood and after. It's a tough job but you can plan a reward to follow. Best of all, though, is knowing that with the second step, building positive new beliefs, you can go on to new heights.

Here, I'm using Jackie's answers as an example; read through to the end to see how she worked things out, then note your own beliefs and your responses to them. You'll find the questions listed for your replies after Jackie's answers.

Old beliefs

What do I believe about myself?

I never get what I want. However hard I try I'll always be lonely and unloved. There's something wrong with me. I can't change. I'm hopeless, useless, unlovable and weird.

How do I know?

I go to places and no one ever talks to me. Mum always told people I'd got nothing to say for myself. She never had time for me. My step-dad didn't want to be with me. Boyfriends either hurt me or leave. People at work laugh and chat but they don't include me. Teachers ignored me.

How do I feel when I think of this?

Hurt, lonely, abandoned, despairing.

How do I expect life to be?

It'll always be the same: OK for everyone but me.

What's the best and the worst that could happen to me?

I'd like to get married and have kids but I'll probably end up a lonely old maid. I'll buy a ground-floor flat and get a dog. I'll die alone. No one will know and the dog will eat me.

How do other people treat me?

They ignore me, put me down or use me. They hurt me and leave me.

How do I behave around other people?

I'm quiet. I never stare because it's rude. I try not to put myself forward. I don't let them find out about me in case I put them off. I try to please them but it's never enough.

Am I important?

No! (Jackie hesitated, then asked, 'Am I supposed to say 'yes'?')

Do I act on my feelings?

No. I don't want to upset people or alienate them. Sometimes, though, I can't help blowing my top and making a fool of myself.

What scenes do I remember that reinforce all this?

Mum telling my cousins, 'Don't mind if Jackie doesn't say anything. She never does.' Her smacking me when she was ironing and I wanted her to play with me. Teachers at school. The girl next door falling out with me and getting her friends to torment me like my stepbrothers did. Alex shushing me because he wanted to watch TV after I'd cleaned his house.

Poor Jackie! No wonder she'd been so unhappy. When she looked at her old beliefs, she found 'proof' that she'd 'never' get what she wanted. Oddly enough, Jackie found some relief in this. It meant she didn't have to face up to her fears. She took comfort from believing she was right so she could keep on repeating what she knew how to do – even though she kept getting the same results. But she didn't want to keep on being stuck. So how did she change her belief system to make her life better?

Build positive new beliefs

Instead of focusing on the painful memories studding her past, Jackie took another sheet of paper and began to note down times when she'd been happy and felt valued even for a moment. She was surprised at how many there were.

What do I believe about myself?

I can learn. I can be good company. I can stick up for myself. I can attract men. Sometimes I get what I want. I'm a good friend. I am good at things. Sometimes I know I'm liked, loved and valued. Not everyone's happy or popular so I'm like other people. I do some things well. I can be likable and valuable.

How do I know?

I learned to walk and talk. I've learned new skills at work. Sometimes I have a laugh. Marie and Leah like me. Ed liked my cooking, Del liked my smile. My neighbours rely on me.

Mum loves me and did her best for me even though she was depressed. I'm good at getting problems sorted in shops. My English teacher had time for me. I talk to my colleagues sometimes. They laugh if I make jokes.

How do I feel when I think of this?

Happier, more relaxed, more confident and optimistic. There are some good things about me!

How do I expect life to be?

I can do different things to make my life better. If I don't automatically keep everyone at a distance I can be close to some of the nice people.

What's the best and the worst that could happen to me?

I could talk to more people and have more friends. I could be more picky and not keep going out with men who hurt me. I could meet someone nice and settle down. I can make the best of things and have fun. Even if things stayed as they are, I can survive because I have done.

How do other people treat me?

Marie, Leah and my neighbours are nice to me. Some of the girls at work talk to me. My supervisor praises me when I do things well. Men chat me up. Mum loves me even if I don't like the way she shows it. Marie's been my friend ever since we met so some people stay with me. My clients like me. Other people are good to me even if my brothers weren't.

How do I behave around other people?

I enjoy talking to my clients and my friends. I can be myself with my friends and neighbours and they still like me. I'm all right making eye contact with them. I can argue with Mum and she always makes up with me.

Am I important?

I'm important to myself because what I do affects me. I'm important to Mum, Marie, Leah, my neighbours and their kids. In some ways I'm important to my clients and colleagues. I helped one of the girls at work so I matter to her.

Do I act on my feelings?

I do sometimes. I dumped Joe when he two-timed me. If I'm nervous about a new task I ask for help. If I'm lonely I can ring a friend.

What scenes do I remember that reinforce all these positives?

Mum helping me set up home. My supervisor being nice sometimes. Going out with Marie and Leah. My neighbours inviting
me round for Christmas. Their kids always hugging me. Alastair
being cuddly and considerate sometimes.

Now that Jackie wasn't screening out the good memories, lots
more came flooding back. There were tears of joy in her eyes as
she told me of them. Are you willing to update your old beliefs
now? Here are those questions again:

Old beliefs
- What do I believe about myself?
- How do I know?
- How do I feel when I think of this?
- How do I expect life to be?
- What's the best and the worst that could happen to me?
- How do other people treat me?
- How do I behave around other people?
- Am I important?
- Do I act on my feelings?
- What scenes do I remember that reinforce all this?

New beliefs
- What do I believe about myself?
- How do I know?
- How do I feel when I think of this?
- How do I expect life to be?
- What's the best and the worst that could happen to me?
- How do other people treat me?
- How do I behave around other people?
- Am I important?
- Do I act on my feelings?
- What scenes do I remember that reinforce all these positives?

Putting your new beliefs into action
If you've gone through those two processes, well done! Why not
celebrate your wonderful new beliefs by destroying the paper that

holds those old ones? You don't need to hang on to them any more, do you? Then enjoy a self-supportive reward. You deserve it!

By the way, imagination is a powerful tool. If you can't think of even one time when someone's smiled at you or been kind, you might enjoy picturing in detail a scene where you fit in and people respond warmly to you. Although she had plenty of good memories, Jackie had a chance to put her imagination to work when she was promoted. Dreading moving to a new office, she discovered that picturing herself behaving in friendly ways towards her new colleagues and their warm response helped her to be confident. She was delighted when her new, more outgoing behaviours got her the acceptance she wanted.

Another way of anchoring your new beliefs in the present is to list your good qualities and skills. You may have fallen for unhelpful messages like 'self-praise is no praise', or the idea that confidence is the same as being boastful, but it isn't. If you're good at something, that's a fact. Boasting would be telling everyone you're better than them but your list is just for you. All you're doing is quietly accepting the truth. As you're important to yourself, you're allowed to use your good points for your own benefit as well as other people's. Why not start your list now?

You can start countering old, unhelpful messages by overlaying positive ones. Some of Jackie's were, 'I'm now allowed to be friendly and outgoing.' 'I'm bubbly and fun to be with.' She didn't feel comfortable with 'I am confident' so she took a step back and said, 'I'm now starting to be confident.' If she still hadn't felt comfortable, she could have said, 'I now want to start learning to be confident' and worked her way up.

These uplifting messages are called affirmations. You phrase them positively and in the present tense. Don't include words like *no*, *less*, *more*, *must* or *ought*. The most effective way of using affirmations is to say them out loud about forty times a day, to your reflection in a mirror. They take about two minutes each. If you do that every day for a fortnight you'll notice the difference.

SUMMARY

By challenging old beliefs with positive facts or fantasies you can update them. Good things count at least as much as bad ones.

Dwelling on good memories and fantasies builds self-esteem. So does acknowledging your good qualities. Act out your new positive beliefs in the present and celebrate each achievement, however small, as a step along your road to confidence.

Part II

You, Your Partner and Your Children

You may want a family of your own. Perhaps you'd just like the support of a partner, preferring to remain child-free. In an over-crowded world this is a valuable option. It's your right to choose. Some people want children, perhaps desperately. Others find they've unwittingly become parents. Let's also not forget that circumstances change so that what starts out as the traditional mum-dad-and-kids situation can alter through bereavement or divorce.

Whatever style of family you want to create, you and your partner will be its architects. If one parent is away from home a lot, for instance through work, ill-health or imprisonment, the parent who is the carer shoulders most of the child-rearing and has to find his or her own support. Alternatively, you may choose to bring up children alone. The absent parent may have been a sperm donor or a partner who's no longer in the central picture. Some women choose to be single mothers, thinking they'll do better if there isn't a man clogging up their lives. They may intend the child to receive valid messages like, 'women are just as good as men' – but as you've seen, the message sent isn't necessarily the one the child takes in. Children of single mothers may end up believing men are never around when you want them. Children of single fathers may believe women are dangerous and unreliable.

Then there's the debate about whether or not mothers should work. If you have big bills there's probably not much choice. Working women might feel guilty that their children are missing out by not having their mothers permanently on tap. Stay-at-home mothers could feel just as guilty because they're not making much financial contribution. They may feel ashamed about finding a two-year-old's babble boring.

However good your intentions are, life can be tough. Outside pressures can mean that parents aren't around as much as they'd like and they're short on energy and patience. But parenting doesn't have to be perfect. Baby **Fred** had a perfect mother. She did everything for him without his having to ask. By the age of four he still wasn't speaking and his mother was demented with worry. The family doctor arranged for hospital tests. His mother became increasingly anxious. Did Fred have brain damage? Was he deaf? The tests showed that Fred was not only normal, but also exceptionally bright. However, the minute he pointed at something his mother rushed to provide it. She guessed his needs and fulfilled them before he said a word. Fred wasn't speaking because he'd never needed to. Perfect parenting means children don't learn to be separate, self-fulfilling individuals.

At the other end of the spectrum there are parents who don't provide adequate nurturing. Perhaps they don't know how to or don't have the strength. If this is the case they can ask for help from their GPs, health centres and baby clinics, experienced friends and relatives, nurseries, childminders and even social services. If you're scared you're an inadequate parent, you're part of a massive club! There's more on overcoming parenting problems in the following chapters, but please be reassured. The authorities would much rather help families stay together than take children away, so it's OK to ask for help. Sometimes parents genuinely don't care. Their child may die of neglect or abuse, or survive despite psychological problems.

In parenting, then, there's one cardinal rule: *good enough is good enough.* But what makes a good parent? What do you need to be one and how can you get it? How can you support your children even through the difficult teenage years – and still stay intact as a happy individual? Even if you don't want children, the advice in this section can still improve your adult relationships and your self-esteem.

Chapter 8

Creating Firm Foundations

You and your partner are the architects of your family, the foundations on which it will rest. Here are some ways to prepare you both for a rewarding future with or without children.

Why are you together?

Why have you and your partner chosen to be a couple? Some parents choose partners for their offspring to cement alliances or add wealth to the family. If that's what you've grown up with, there's nothing wrong with it – so long as you and your partner are reasonably happy together. *You* are the judge of whether you're happy enough to make your relationship worthwhile.

In technologically advanced societies love is the main reason couples form. Songs, films and adverts all promote the loving couple as the norm. My husband and I are together because we love each other and we're happy. Unfortunately, love can be both good and bad. Good love is stable and secure. The two of you support and respect each other. You genuinely like each other's company. You trust each other and feel wholly accepted. You're lovers as well as best friends but you also allow each other freedom, knowing it won't be abused.

It's easy, however, to mistake sexual attraction for love. Great sex is no guarantee that you'll be happy together out of bed. Although this may come as a surprise to teenagers, the average person spends less than 2 per cent of their life having sex. That's why it's worth taking time to make sure you're compatible in practical and emotional terms before embarking on a sexual relationship – because sex can mean babies and that changes your life.

'If only' relationships are common too. Fancying someone from afar isn't love. It's infatuation. Even within marriage an 'if only' mindset leaves one person desperately clinging on, trying to excuse or blank out uncomfortable behaviours and perhaps feeling guilty that they're upset or scared.

So what has all this to do with the family you want to create? Simply this: if a couple don't get on well, having children won't bind them together. The additional stresses of family life pull shaky couples apart. The whole subject of children and how to bring them up is one of the 'big four' causes of arguments. (In case you're interested, the other three are money, chores and sex – which are also affected by having children.)

There are whole books on building a good relationship with your-self and then with your partner (*see* Resources, *page 202*). The most important part is selecting a partner who wants what you do and who's as glad to be with you as you are with them. Assuming you've got that part sorted, let's concentrate on the parenthood aspect.

If you and your partner have different views on being a parent, isn't it better to iron them out *before* you bring a flesh-and-blood child into the equation? If your beloved doesn't want children but you do, are you really right for each other? Wouldn't each of you (and any children) be better off with someone whose life plan is closer to yours? And what would you do if one of you was found to be infertile? There'd be fewer divorces if couples thrashed all this out before they got married.

Even if you've already got children it can be a very useful exercise to compare what you and your partner think about kids, parenting and parents' respective roles. People aren't always aware of the discrepancies between what they *think* they do and what they *actually* do. Even in the best-regulated households things don't always go the way you expect. No one *plans* for illness, money troubles or any of the other problems that can strike, but it's important for each partner to let the other know what's going on for them and what they need at any given time. This know-ledge can be essential in supporting each other, not least so the children don't run rings around you.

Minimising family friction is one reason for talking these ideas through. Another is to set up a helpful framework for solving problems with the least amount of trouble. Discussions can strengthen your relationship – so long as you realise that your partner has a right to her opinion even if it's not the same as yours. The single exception is where one parent's views put the children at risk – because above all, having children is a huge responsibility, and one that lasts for decades. When you're dead and gone, what will your children think of you?

The case against having children

I love children. I wouldn't be without my daughter, but I know plenty of people who have thoroughly regretted becoming parents. Here's one example.

On a train one day I met a man I'll call **Darren**. He said, 'Babies are loud, smelly and expensive. Teenagers are loud, argumentative and even more expensive. Before we married my wife talked about wanting kids but she knew I didn't. She promised she'd stay on the Pill but she lied about taking it. One sprog I might have coped with, but three times she got pregnant and expected me to be pleased. I haven't slept with her for eleven years because it's just too big a risk. Now I've got to stump up for two kids at college and a daughter who wants a big wedding. I hate going back to all the sulks and demands and rows if I won't give in. It doesn't feel like my home at all. It's theirs. She's poisoned them against me. Mostly they ignore me unless they want something. My wife's just this harassed nag I pass in the hall. I haven't seen the gorgeous, smiling woman I fell in love with for years. Now I dream of escaping abroad and changing my name so they can't find me. If I could afford it I'd get a divorce. Can you blame me for having affairs?'

I don't know what happened after Darren got off the train but it doesn't sound like a story with a happy ending. I'd hate to live in that house too. Wouldn't you? I feel so sorry for all of them: the unwilling father who's reduced to a cash-cow, the lonely mother trying to hold it all together and the children who despise their father. Every one of them feels betrayed.

Children do cost money. At the time of going to press you'd be lucky to have change out of £35,000 for each child you rear from birth to the age of eighteen. You'd have to budget for a lot more if you're going to pay for your children's way through college or help with a wedding. They also cost one parent at least four months' loss of earnings and possibly much more. Childcare can cost most of one parent's wage. (Though you might get benefits to help: ask the Citizens Advice Bureau or your Neighbourhood Office for details.)

Unless you leave them to a nanny, children also take up time – you have to nurture them, educate them and play with them. Spending time with the children means less time for yourself, your partner and your social life.

Having children takes energy. Imagine strapping sixteen pounds of potatoes to your body day and night for four or five months! Labour is called that because it's hard work. It usually hurts and can take hours or even days. Many mothers don't recover physically from the birth for six to twelve months. Children have to be lifted and carried, changed, washed, dressed and fed. It's exhausting. Try doing all that with a full-time job! Yet thousands of women do. Where will you keep the baby-bath, the nappies, the cot, the clothes, the bottles and sterilisers and toys? Who'll look after these things?

Having children limits your freedom. Lots of people imagine they'll still enjoy the same active social life as they did before they had children. But it's hard to be spontaneous with children. Even if you can afford a childminder you trust, you've got to find one who's available or take the child with you. The amount of paraphernalia you need for a day out is surprising. Child-free friends may lose contact. And what if you embark on an evening's romance only to find that your toddler is sick?

Even the healthiest of children have nightmares. And colds. And stomach upsets. And teething troubles. For at least the first few years sleeping through the night is a bonus to be thankful for. Unless your childminder has no other children to take care of (unlikely), you'll need time off work for medical appointments. And what if (God forbid) your child has a more serious health problem? How will you cope?

Don't forget the emotional drain. There probably isn't a parent alive who hasn't worried about their child at least some

of the time. Bearing and caring for a child can play havoc with
your hormones and therefore your moods. Many mothers say
their womb still hurts if their baby cries – and children do cry,
sometimes for hours. Imagine how helpless you'd feel if you'd
done everything you could think of and your offspring was still
howling. Frustration with prolonged wailing is one of the most
common triggers for child abuse. I doubt whether there's a
parent who hasn't had an argument with their child, or disapproved of at least one aspect of his behaviour. And then he grows
up and leaves.

The case for having children

While all of the above is true, people still go on having children
on purpose. For most people the pleasures far outweigh the pain.
That's why so many grandmothers go gaga over babies: they can
relive all the good bits without the 24/7 drawbacks.

If you're lucky, being a parent is one of the most rewarding
and fulfilling things in life (although there are plenty of others).
Seeing your child develop is a source of happiness and pride.
The milestones stick in your memory: his first word, her first steps,
the parties, the holidays, the triumphs in school and out of it. It's
fantastic playing and reading with your children. You'll probably
end up with a houseful of hand-drawn birthday cards and wobbly
presents they've made you. No words can describe the intense
joy of being close to your children. The special moments really
are special – particularly in contrast to the less-than-wonderful
bits! Many factors are involved in different people's decision to
have children:

- For some parenthood is bound up with the biological impera-
  tive: species reproduce in order to survive. It's why women in
  their thirties might talk about their biological clock ticking.
  Women, after all, are more closely concerned since they're
  designed to carry, give birth to and suckle the child. Some men
  also care about fulfilling their role as a step on the evolutionary
  ladder.
- Some women positively enjoy the glow of pregnancy. Some are
  lucky enough even to enjoy childbirth.

- There can be social prompts. Landed gentry were until recently expected to provide heirs for the family fortune. Versions of this social requirement still survive.
- Some intellectual types want to pass on their intelligence so it's not lost to society.
- Sometimes 'our kind of people' want offspring so that 'our' values outweigh 'theirs' in the world.
- Relatives may put pressure on couples to reproduce, perhaps saying there's something wrong with people who don't have children. Given that the global population is doubling every thirty-two years, isn't it time to confront that archaic belief?
- In some cultures having many children adds status.
- Children may be borne so that they can look after their parents in their old age.
- Some leaders of the two fastest growing religions teach their followers to have as many children as possible 'for the faith'.
- Accidents do happen. Though contraception is widely available in the West, women do get pregnant without meaning to. Many decide to keep the child in spite of the potential problems.

Potentially dangerous reasons for having children
If you or your partner are contemplating having children for any of the reasons below you could be heading for trouble.

So you won't be alone
Children grow up. From around eight or nine they'll increasingly want friends and lives of their own. Wanting them always to be with you is selfish and can damage them emotionally. Why not make friends? Improve your adult relationships? Do something for your community? Invest in your career? Find other healthy ways of having fun? Don't you want your children to respect as well as love you?

To please your parents
If you're still trying to please your parents you've probably realised they're so demanding it's never going to happen. They've had their chance. Their lives and emotions are their responsibility. You're allowed to live your own life the way you choose.

To get state benefits
This is largely a myth but it has been known. Using a child as a tool to manipulate others can work in the short term but then you're left holding the baby. You'll have to take care of her for at least sixteen years.

To cement your relationship with your partner
It won't. Even if you stay in the same house the added stresses will make things more uncomfortable, not less. Having children drives shaky couples apart.

To 'get it right this time'
Many couples want to do things differently from their parents. That's OK. But if that's your main motivation for having children, it's not really the child's well-being that matters, is it? Do you think that's fair on someone who didn't ask to be born?

So why do you want children?
Wanting a child can be an almost overwhelming urge. What, then, is the point of all this talk?

It's because children are important. They're the continuation of humanity and its hope for better things. They're also dependent and vulnerable and they deserve the best start in life possible. Isn't it sensible to make plans that will benefit parents and children alike?

We all think our own ideas are the most realistic view of how the world works. The ideas we each grew up with probably seem normal to us. Unfortunately, it's easy to assume your partner's views will match your own, which can lead to some nasty surprises. Counsellors meet some of the victims of those surprises, but many people are too afraid to go and see a counsellor.

Here are some of the questions you may want to resolve with your partner before you embark on the pleasures and perils of parenthood.

What are your reasons for having children?
- Is it important to you to have children? Why?
- What do you want them for?
- How many do you want?

- How will you arrange to have (only) that many?
- At what point in your lives do you want children?
- Do you associate not having children with failure?

How will you cope with problems?
- How do you feel about contraception and sterilisation?
- How would you cope with not conceiving, miscarriage, stillbirth or infant death?
- What will you do if you can't have children?
- Apart from having children (or not), what matters to you? How else will you find fulfilment? (This one is very important. Please take your time discussing it!)
- How will you resolve difficulties or differing viewpoints?

How will you nurture your relationship with your partner?
- What do you want from each other to add to your happiness?
- How will you arrange time out for the parent who stays with the child?
- And for the one who goes to work?
- How can you maintain your loving relationship when you have children?

What is each parent supposed to do?
- What do you think a mother's role is?
- And a father's?
- Who'll get up to see to the child in the night?
- Who'll take time off if the child is ill?
- How will you divide the chores?
- How will you handle a child who keeps crying?
- How will you show your children you love and value them?
- Will you bring the children up according to any religious practices?
- What behaviours don't you want them to see?
- What do you want to protect them from?
- Will you both take responsibility for discipline?
- What will you punish your children for, and how?
- What subjects (if any) won't you discuss in front of them at different ages?

- Do you believe in admitting to children that you've made a mistake? Will you apologise?
- Do you have ambitions for them?
- What will you do if the children don't share your ambitions?
- How will you react if your child doesn't have the sexual orientation you'd prefer?

How will having children fit in with the rest of your life?
- Which is more important, work or family?
- Who (if anyone) is the most important person in your family?
- How will you finance your life with children?
- How will you divide spending money for each partner?
- When do you the think the mother/father should go back to work?

What are your children supposed to do?
- What views of gender stereotyping do you want your child to display?
- What freedoms (including driving) should the children be allowed at different ages?
- What attitudes do you want them to grow up with? (For example towards money, gambling, sex, religion, education, respect for others, animals, loyalty versus individuality, honesty, courage and safety, family life, relatives, friends, work, leisure, health, tobacco, alcohol and other drugs.)
- Should working children pay board?
- At what age do you think your children should leave home?

SUMMARY
Children are important but also fragile and vulnerable. Parents are responsible for them until they reach adulthood. Sharing attitudes to parenting and parent roles sets the framework for the family you create. It minimises friction and gives you a rough road map of where you want each of the people in your family to go and how you'd like them to get there. As you, your partner and your children are all individuals, things probably won't always go according to plan. It's OK to be flexible, to admit to mistakes and make changes.

Chapter 9

Challenging Negative Thinking

Have you ever felt you can't cope? These helpful permissions could be your first step towards overcoming depression and anxiety.

How are you coping?
Pressure can come at you from any direction. Health, money, work, friends and, of course, family are just some of the areas that can trigger problems. Even positive life changes can knock you off balance for a while. Whatever the source of your stress, there are two factors to deal with: the practical difficulties and your emotional response. How you feel naturally affects how you cope. The techniques you'll find here for managing stress can be applied in any situation. But as this section also has parenting as its theme, I'm using an example of stress based on the arrival of a first child. If you'd like to find more positive ways of dealing with any kind of pressure, read on.

Stress and the first child
Claire hadn't wanted to admit to anyone that she was stressed by daughter **Zoe**. Between a difficult birth and a demanding baby, Claire was mentally and physically exhausted. Her concentration was poor and her mood fragile. Her temper was on a hair-trigger and she and husband **Nick** were having horrible arguments. Both felt criticised, unloved and unappreciated. They guiltily resented the baby who'd created such chaos in their previously loving home. But it was Claire's unhappy feelings of being trapped and inadequate that prompted her health visitor to recommend counselling.

Here's what Claire learned about how to handle stress. If you'd like to manage stress in a way that's more supportive for yourself, this could be just what you need.

Stress and your thinking

Coping with any major life change is bound to call for some adjustment. Whatever causes the external pressure, the principles underlying internal stress responses are the same. Many people mistakenly believe that the situation leads directly to the feeling. It doesn't. Different people react to the same event in very different ways. Take redundancy. Individuals' responses include suicide; depression; ill-health; vengeful anger; a matter-of-fact determination to find a better boss; excitement at new opportunities; and a sense of joyous liberation. In reality, the biggest factor in how you feel is what you *think* about a situation.

Prolonged negative thinking lowers the amount of feel-good hormones your body produces. It also shrinks the receptors in your brain so even fewer feel-good hormones are usefully absorbed. The positive intention behind this is to focus your mind on your problems so that you solve them. After all, if a rhino were charging at you, stopping to smell the pretty flowers wouldn't help you survive. But in today's society, the adrenaline surge that would help you focus on responding constructively to a rhino's charge isn't always helpful. Most of our problems can't be solved by fighting or running away. That means the adrenaline isn't burned up by physical activity so instead it can stay sloshing around in our systems, keeping us focused on the source of our anxiety. The stress response becomes a new event, to which you react by producing more adrenaline, which increases your anxiety, and so on. You can end up thinking in circles, as though you were stuck on a treadmill. You may believe you've done everything you can to solve the problem, but it doesn't mean you've done everything there is. Let's see how Claire began to overcome her spiralling panic.

Identify your negative thoughts

Claire began to separate out *facts* from *thinking*. The facts were:

Having just moved to a new area, Clare felt isolated. As a new mother she'd decided to stay at home with her child, so finding friends and self-esteem through work weren't viable options right now. Zoe was a demanding child who didn't sleep much. Claire hadn't settled into a routine. Without her income, money was tight. Nick was behaving in hostile ways and offering little emotional support. Her parents were too far away to offer much practical help and her mother was often critical.

Like Claire did (*see above*), you could write down the *facts* of your situation by putting it in the third person (*he* and *she* rather than *I*) and avoiding any mention of feelings or value judgements. That's the first step.

When Claire expressed her story using the first person (*I*) and included feelings, thought distortions became apparent. I've put them in *italics* in the story below. These distortions, rather than the situation itself, were what she had largely been responding to, as you'll see.

Everything seems so hopeless. I shouldn't feel this way. Everyone else can manage fine but I'm useless. I can't do anything right. I feel so *trapped* and *helpless. I'll never be able to sort this out.* Nick is *always* angry with me. *I'm ruining his life because I'm not good enough. Nobody cares about me. Mum's always bossing me about and criticising me. I can't ask anyone for help.* I'm scared *I'll never be able to cope* and *things will always be like this. I'll always be lonely* because *no one would want to be friends with a bad mother like me.*

Comparing the two versions, you'll see that Claire's feelings were distorting her interpretation of the facts. Repeating these self-defeating beliefs, she felt even more trapped, helpless and so on. So what could she do to counter these negative thoughts and start finding solutions so she felt better?

Putting negative thoughts into perspective

I invited Claire to give herself the following permissions and see how she could apply them to her situation. You'll see below what they are and how they helped her find better coping strategies that in turn lifted her mood. After her example you'll find the permissions listed again for you to use if you want to.

I'm allowed to exist

I existed quite happily before Zoe or Nick came along. I'm entitled to have a life now as well. Even if Nick and I split up I'll survive and so will Zoe. Other divorcees learn how to manage independently, so I could too.

It's OK to be me. I'm a separate individual

It's not my fault Zoe cries a lot. I don't have to accept Nick's and Mum's criticisms or blame that isn't mine. I'm not responsible for how Nick feels. He's equally accountable for the decision to have Zoe. Other women have problems too, so it's not just me. No one is perfect, and I don't have to be either. Back home I have lots of friends and people who appreciate me. My worth doesn't depend only on my mothering skills (which I'm improving anyway). I have useful skills and interests and I can use them for myself too.

I am important

I'm important to myself because I live through my own senses. My actions affect me more than anyone else. I'm important to Zoe. She wouldn't have survived or exist at all without me. I'm important to my old friends. (When Claire eventually asked Nick, he confirmed she was important to him too.) My parents are critical because they love me and want me to be successful, well and happy.

I can feel what I feel

My feelings, even the uncomfortable ones, give me the information I need to start solving problems. I can find more positive ways to act on my feelings.

I can think well and clearly (including getting information I need) to solve problems

I'm keeping Zoe and myself alive so I'm doing OK and I can learn to do better. When I feel lonely, I can go to places where I can meet other people and make new friends. I can ask Nick to mind Zoe sometimes while I go for a walk. I asked the health visitor for advice, and that's a good coping strategy. I can ask Nick why he's so grouchy. Maybe together we can sort things out. If negative thoughts come to mind I can challenge them or think about something else.

I can be grown up and handle adult situations well

I don't have to do everything all on my own. I can ask for help if I want to. I'm doing quite well with the housework even though

I don't like it and I'm doing very well with the garden. It's adult to recognise my good qualities. It's adult to realise Nick can't fulfil all my emotional needs, but friends and others could help.

I can be successful

Some days I feel reasonably in control. There are plenty of things I've learned to be good at so I'll be good at this being a wife and mother once I'm used to it. Zoe smiles at me and misses me if I'm not there so I'm not that bad a mother. I made good friendships before so I can again.

I can have fun

Money's tight but I can watch comedy programmes on TV, ring my old friends or write to them, or do an art class at the adult education centre if it has a creche. I sometimes have fun playing with Zoe, so I'll make more time for that. I'll do my hobbies while Zoe's asleep. Sometimes I have a laugh with Nick.

I can be well and sane

I haven't always felt this bad. I'm starting to feel well and sane again. Things will get better as I get better, and vice versa.

I can be close when I choose to be

Sometimes I feel resentful because Zoe's so invasive and demanding but sometimes it's lovely to cuddle her and play with her. I can make friends with people who aren't critical. If Mum or Nick criticises unfairly, I don't have to accept that. Sometimes it's nice making love with Nick. I can snuggle up to him when he's asleep even if he's sometimes stand-offish when he's awake.

I can belong

I did feel I belonged with my friends and colleagues. Sometimes I felt safe and included when I lived at home with Mum and Dad. I do belong with Nick and Zoe.

There's one other permission that Zoe didn't need, but you might. It's *You can take action*. If you grew up with parents who wrapped you in cotton wool, you might feel scared to take positive actions for fear that something terrible will happen. So long as you work out sensible precautions, checking them out with someone you like and trust if you choose to, you can act in ways that are self-supportive and respectful of yourself and others.

The Results

Now you've read through those permissions with Claire's examples, how do you feel about them? If any of them sound too challenging right now, you could talk them through with a therapist, your doctor or a friend, or you could come back to them when you're ready to. Shortly you'll see them again for your own use, but let's find out how this exercise worked for Claire.

Claire wrote down the headings of those permissions and carried them around to read often. Over the next few weeks she discovered that she now felt able to resolve problems rather than merely feeling stuck and overwhelmed. This meant she also felt better about herself. As Claire's stress levels dropped, she approached Zoe in a more positive way and Zoe responded more positively too, so the tensions at home began to dissolve. Now Claire wasn't blaming herself entirely for the problems with Nick, she told him what had worked for her. It was up to him whether he'd do the same.

Here are those permissions again for you:

• I'm allowed to exist.
• It's OK to be me. I'm a separate individual.
• I am important.
• I can feel what I feel.
• I can think well and clearly (including getting information I need) to solve problems.
• I can be grown up and handle adult situations well.
• I can be successful.
• I can have fun.
• I can be well and sane.
• I can be close when I choose to be.
• I can belong.
• I can take action.

You and your partner

In theory, after yourself, the next person you can rely on for support is your partner. In practice it doesn't always work out that way because your partner may be suffering from thought distortions and stresses of his own. In a joint session we discovered what was going on for Claire's husband Nick. What he thought is common in new fathers. Once again I'll put into *italics* the thought distortions and mistaken beliefs that had left him feeling hostile.

Now I've given a bit of sperm she doesn't need me. I could die tomorrow and they'd go on *quite happily* without me. *She thinks more of Zoe than she does of me* because if she cries Claire just leaves me to go to her, and she *never* wants sex any more. *All I am is a meal ticket* but *that's pointless* because she always earned a bigger salary than me. I worry *no end* about money and I'm *always* exhausted but *she doesn't care, she just wants more and more from me. I can't stand her and Zoe crying. She must hate me.* I *just* want to get away because *I can't cope.*

Poor Nick! And poor Claire! The two of them, exhausted by their new responsibilities, had both tried to hide their anxieties and so had cut off from each other. Having heard his side of things in a session, Claire reassured him that she loved and needed him and that he mattered to her as much as he ever had. She was grateful for his financial support, and sad not to have more time and energy for him. She'd been scared he no longer loved her because she hadn't felt good enough for him.

Nick guiltily admitted he'd felt the same. To compensate, he'd been trying to copy his father (who hadn't talked intimately to Nick as a child) presuming that was a good role model. But of course parents share deeper ideas with their partner than with young offspring. Nick felt sheepish but relieved when he realised this. They fell into each other's arms. I was very touched as they reaffirmed their love.

Over the next few weeks Nick also took the permissions he needed: to exist as his own valuable self; to know he was still important and that he belonged with Claire and Zoe and could be close to them; to share his feelings and thinking so they could work things out together; to know he was successful as a husband and parent as well as a colleague; and to let himself be open with friends.

Nick and Claire combined their resources. They worked out ways to help each other and planned one special evening a week, even if it was only to have a meal and a bottle of wine at home, but they also joined a baby-sitting circle so they could go out together once in a while.

The moral of this is that your partner's motives for hostility or withholding support may not be the ones you fear. It makes sense, then, to share your *feelings* and the reasons you feel that way, not blamefully but using the Emotional Literacy techniques you've already learned in the first section. Once you both know what's going on in the emotional department, you can combine your *thinking* to plan a course of *action*.

Now, though, let's see how you can use your joint resources to prevent or minimise stress before it has a chance to take hold on your children. After all, changes in the structure of the family are stressful for children too, and they don't have your adult coping mechanisms. Although I'm using the birth of a second child as an example of how children might experience stress, the same techniques of *open communication* can profitably be applied to help children conquer stress in other situations.

Your other children

Here's the inspiring story of **Pat** and **Mary** and their two year old, **Sean**, when baby **Gerarda** was born.

Around the age of two children start to separate out emotionally from the mother who up to now has been the centre of their world. You'll see them go off exploring, then dashing back to make sure their mother is still there. This urge for individuation also prompts them to start saying 'no' to their parents as they learn their limits and limitations. They want to form a bond with their father, partly out of competition for the mother's attention and partly because the father offers different possibilities.

At the same time the 'terrible twos' are when children have night terrors. Unable to distinguish clearly between reality, dreams and imagination, they're unsure of the extent of their power. They may wish angrily that their mother would disappear and stop spoiling their fun, but if she does they get scared if they can't instantly find her again. Have they made her vanish? Is it their fault she's gone? Have they been abandoned? Is it because there's something wrong with them? If the mother does leave them for a while, even to go to the toilet, they often feel hurt, betrayed or insecure, and when she gets back they may be angry at her for causing such bad feelings. As you can imagine, learning to cope with all this makes for a lot of big tasks to learn for a person whose ability to form, verbalise and compare ideas is so restricted.

Then along comes another baby, fragile and demanding, getting between them and the centre of their world. Stress seems inevitable. Here's how Mary's family successfully helped Sean handle the new arrival. As far as possible I'll present it from Sean's point of view.

Mum had gone into hospital to give birth, taking the foundations of Sean's world with her. He knew where she was and why Dad was with her, but he was still anxious away from them. Although he loved Grandma, who was around a lot more these days, she wasn't the same. Why couldn't everything go back to the way it used to be?

Sean felt important and clever, though, because a few weeks back Mum and Dad had explained about having the new baby. When baby Gerarda was born, Sean liked the present they gave him to celebrate her birth, and Grandma spent plenty of time with him. Dad was still working, so Sean was used to him being away and coming back. They'd started Sean at playgroup so he could learn to tolerate his mother's absences. He felt very important telling his friends about their baby. Dad took him to see his mother and baby sister in hospital, making sure Gerarda was in her cot so Sean could cuddle his mum, and then letting him hold Gerarda while encircled by his mother's arms.

Back home he did feel a bit pushed out at times, especially after Grandma left. He often came into Mum and Dad's bed for a cuddle, then one of them would carry him back to his room and sing to him until he fell asleep. For a while he went back to his dummy and needed nappies again like the baby did. Mum didn't tell him off. She just gave him lots of praise when he used the potty. Slowly he forgot his dummy. Once he even crept into Gerarda's room and pinched her because he was angry. She cried and Mum was very cross. She smacked Sean's hand and said he mustn't hurt Gerarda, but then gave him lots of cuddles and said, 'You're my special, good, kind boy that I love. I couldn't manage without you.'

Sean felt very grown up helping to look after his sister and tidying up. At night sometimes Mum gave him his bath and sometimes Dad did. Sean would snuggle with Gerarda on a lap while he had his story and she had her bottle. Gerarda smelled nice and held his hand. Mum said Gerarda didn't mean to pull his hair and showed him how to peel the baby's hand away gently, giving her a finger to hold instead.

One day Sean was very angry. He didn't like walking around the supermarket. He wanted to be the one Mum pushed around in the trolley. Then she wouldn't let him take some sweets at the checkout. He knew Mum and Dad sometimes made him do what they wanted by being angry. He threw himself down, screaming, kicking and banging his head on the floor to show he was angry too.

Mum just ignored him and walked away despite a well-meaning old lady saying she was cruel. Sean jumped up and ran after Mum, smiling so she'd like him again. Outside the shop she gave him a big hug as she lifted him into the buggy. He did have a few more tantrums, banging his head on the wall of the lounge, but Mum just carried him over to by the sofa where he couldn't hurt himself and left him to it. When he stopped she made a fuss of him and played games until he was in fits of giggles.

SUMMARY

Each member of the family will experience stress but by sharing your *feelings* and the reasons for them, you and your partner can combine your *thinking* and decide on a positive plan of action. By giving yourself and your child useful permissions you can combat thought distortions and so minimise stress responses. If you have problems you can get help by asking for it. While your family is one support network you, your partner and your child need others too.

Chapter 10

Building Your Confidence and Managing Children's Behaviour

Has it been hard to balance discipline with love? Here are some positive strategies for managing your children's behaviour – and your own.

Giving and getting attention

Everyone needs attention sometimes. If ever a friend of yours has walked past you without at least saying hello you probably felt puzzled. She probably just didn't see you, but you may be worried you'd somehow upset her. It's nice when people acknowledge your existence. Even a smile in passing helps you feel validated. It's something from outside that breaks into your internal world and lets you know you're real.

People need attention. You may remember pictures of the Rumanian orphans whose nurses had no time to interact with them. They'd sit and bang their heads on their cot bars. Lacking outside stimulation, this was how they gave attention to themselves. Human hunger for recognition and stimulation is so strong that if you can't reliably get the pleasant variety, the negative kind is an essential substitute. Without it you'd have serious problems relating to yourself and the world, or even surviving.

The most intense form of recognition is touch. As a child your existence depended on people handling you to take care of you, so touch symbolised staying alive. If the touch was loving you had extra reassurance that you were welcome in the world. That's why Transactional Analysts call units of attention *strokes*.

Growing up, humans learn to appreciate symbolic recognition. A wave or a phone call can leave you feeling good about yourself. If you remember a pleasant conversation, you can renew your good feelings about these symbolic strokes.

Because attention is vital to survival and well-being, everyone develops strategies for getting it. These strategies together can be called the Stroke Economy. If you can't rely on positive strokes when you're young, you're likely to set up unconsciously to get negatives strokes instead, and to mistrust positive strokes. I vividly remember as a young teacher telling a lad, 'That's excellent work.' He instantly replied, 'No it's not!' I smiled and reassured him he really had done very well. He shot to his feet, yelling, 'I don't want your lies!' Tearing up his work, he threw it in my face and ran out of the classroom. He found positive attention, even though it was sincere, too much of a challenge to his view of himself and his place in the world. When he did return to school, he would deliberately spoil his work, telling me, 'See? I told you I was useless!'

Once you know about it, you can use the Stroke Economy effectively to combine love and discipline. It could help you build confidence in yourself and other family members. Let's see how that worked for **Vivian,** whose story goes from tragedy to success. She's living proof that by changing your Stroke Economy you can make life better for yourself and your family.

Living by the need for attention

Viv was fourteen when I first met her. Before her teens she had been smart and well behaved, yet now she was scruffy and constantly in trouble. Once she'd dreamed of becoming a doctor, but now she'd dropped into low-ability sets where she messed around and under-performed. She hung around with scapegoats and vandals. She bit her nails until they bled and carved her boyfriend's name into her arm with a razor blade. She left school at sixteen, drifting into various boring jobs.

When Viv became pregnant her boyfriend dumped her. She had an abortion, fell pregnant to another lad and was brutally thrown out by her father until she had another termination. Then she fell in love with **Eddie**. She ran away with him and had two children, **Joshua** and **Alice**. Even though Eddie got drunk and beat her black and blue, she depended on his sporadic affection and loved him too much to leave him. She added a qualifier: if Eddie hurt the children she'd take them away like a shot. There's more about Viv's story in a minute. Let's now have a look at the ideas that had got her into this mess.

In the family where Viv grew up, she'd learned some pretty damaging beliefs through experience, by observing her parents and three brothers, and by making the sorts of decisions about herself to which children are prone. Her Life Position was I-U+ and she acted out a *never* script. The family Scapegoat, she'd accepted many of the distorted messages you encountered in the last chapter, and such family rules as 'girls aren't important and shouldn't express any emotions apart from happiness'. She'd developed a Stroke Economy based on negative attention. Its tenets were:

I can't get or trust positive attention

Viv had tried to please her parents, kept the family rules, worked diligently and helped her mother at home. As a child she'd stayed in at their insistence. On one level that was for her own protection, but the effect was to isolate her so her family was her main source of attention. This monopoly of the Stroke Economy helped her family maintain their power over her.

However hard she tried, though, Viv's parents wouldn't accept that she was good enough, not least because she wasn't a boy. To teenage Viv the solution was obvious: what she could rely on was negative attention. After all, that was what she got when she struggled to do her best, so why take such pains if no reward was forthcoming? Viv's poor behaviour invited teachers' criticism. If anyone praised her she thought they were lying. Now she was labelled a 'bad girl', only 'bad boys' would pay her attention. Although boys ignored, used or mistreated her sometimes, if one of them paid her positive attention she could sometimes feel loved and valued, which certainly hadn't seemed possible at home.

Viv's parents were not monsters. Although they were far stricter with her than with her brothers their intentions were good. They gave her a home, food, clothes, presents and holidays. However, both parents believed boys were more important so Viv felt neglected emotionally. On rare occasions the harassed father would take out his bad temper on Viv and her mother. They accepted this as normal. Poor Viv had cups, coat hangers and even chairs flung at her. Although this didn't happen often the father always blamed Viv for 'making' him do it. And let's not forget that Viv's 'nice' top-set school-friends had also abandoned her.

I can't reject attention I don't want

Viv didn't actually like her father and big brothers hurting and belittling her, but she only stopped them by running away. When she did do her homework the gang at school trashed it and she was powerless to prevent teachers from punishing her. When the 'nice' girls were spiteful to her she didn't know how to stop them. To keep in with the gang she had to pretend she was amused by their unkind pranks. She felt unable to reject the attentions of lads who used and abandoned her, and she couldn't stop Eddie abusing her. Because she felt dependent on him for any positive attention at all, she clung to him. This sent the message that she accepted his cruelty.

I can't ask for attention when I want it

Loving reassurance wasn't part of the family culture. Viv's two older brothers bullied her to fit in with their dad. Her youngest brother was good to her in secret but dared not show it where the others could see. While her mother didn't actually persecute her, she was scared of allying with Viv in case she too was made a scapegoat.

I can't give strokes when I want to

Viv certainly wasn't allowed to give her family 'Keep off!' messages. When she tried to be friendly with her former 'nice' friends they'd ignore or make fun of her. When she wanted to show affection to her boyfriends she was often pushed away.

I can't give myself positive attention

Viv distrusted praise and kindness from others. She'd come to regard herself as someone who only deserved bad treatment and couldn't get any other kind – hence the painful nail biting. The self-mutilation consisting of carving a boy's name on her arm was intended to reinforce the positive message that she belonged with him. She'd mistakenly been taught that it was big-headed to acknowledge her good points. Even when she tried to give herself positive strokes, it was in self-damaging ways.

If these rules about attention invite hurt, what promotes happiness instead?

Positive ways of getting and giving attention

Viv is now a well-groomed woman approaching thirty. In a drunken rage one night, Eddie had broken her jaw. In hospital she finally realised she couldn't ignore her suffering even if the children weren't at physical risk because if things got worse she might not be able to look after them. She got the number of Women's Aid from a poster and soon accepted places for herself, Josh and Alice in a distant refuge where she had counselling. She's never looked back. Since the children started school she's got a good job that offers training. She, nine-year-old Josh and six-year-old Alice live in a sunny apartment with a garden. They're generally happy, openly affectionate and at ease with each other and their friends.

Viv has decided ideas about bringing up her kids with mutual respect and loving acceptance. Her basic precepts for her children and herself are about giving and withholding strokes. Here's the updated Stroke Economy she uses:

- There's plenty of positive attention to go around. The more you give, the more you're likely to get.
- I can give positive or negative strokes when I want to.
- I can ask for positive strokes.
- I can accept positive attention when I want to.
- I can reject attention I don't want.
- I can give myself positive attention.

Viv includes negative attention so she can set limits with other adults and with her children. They need to learn what's acceptable behaviour. When a male colleague once sexually harassed her, she said loudly, 'Stop touching me like that!' She's also told Josh, 'I don't like it when you hide Alice's dolls. It's unkind.' The explanations help her children take responsibility for their actions and consequences. Then she might sit the offender up to the table or send him to his room and make him stay there until he apologises. She might withdraw a privilege such as watching a favourite TV programme, or withhold pocket money.

Viv gives her children plenty of positive attention because she knows from experience that if parents give mostly negative strokes children are likely to tune their parents out. Anyway, hugs and kindness create a much nicer atmosphere as well as showing children they're valuable and lovable. Because Viv mostly shows her love in ways *that feel good to them*, they're loving to her too. She often gives praise, but only when it's genuine. Praising something that doesn't merit it doesn't teach value. Now Viv doesn't set herself up to get negative attention and can reject it if she wants, she's happier and more confident. See if you can set up to be similarly happier too.

Types of attention

Attention, both negative and positive, comes in different types. For a start you have touch, words and symbolic attention such as letters or presents. Cuddles and sitting close to your child show him he belongs, that he's important and likable. Listening to your child with interest, playing together or sharing activities with him is validating. A child who can say to you, 'I want a hug' knowing that she'll get one is more confident than child who cannot do this.

Attention can be unconditional. 'I hate you!' condemns the listener wholly. 'I love you' is positive and unconditional. Conditional attention focuses on one aspect of the person. 'I like your hair like that' is a conditional positive. 'You need a bath' is a conditional negative.

So how can you use this to manage a child's behaviour or your own? It's helpful to label the situation rather than yourself or the child. Then you can concentrate on the solution. Say your child has a runny nose. Yelling, 'You're disgusting!' condemns the child globally and doesn't say what behaviour you want changed. 'Let me wipe your nose' is a caring request that specifically addresses the behaviour.

Children who've internalised a lot of negative messages find it hard to accept positives. If you tell a child who thinks he's stupid, 'You're clever,' your positive message will probably backfire, as you've seen. However, if you use a conditional negative like 'Not bad!' or a back-handed compliment like 'You did that quite well considering,' he'll find it less confrontational and will be more inclined to accept it. This is a step on the way to him learning to accept unconditional praise.

People are unlikely to make overnight changes in their stroking patterns. Having built up their own model for getting attention, those who've learned to rely on negatives will take some time to accept that they can now get – and trust – positives. Many's the classroom rebel whose parents have despaired of his future, only to find that once he leaves school he settles down. This is partly because he's no longer in an environment where he expects – and sets up to get – negative strokes. And, of course, choosing what you do is far more rewarding than reluctant obedience.

If you or your children have been setting up to get negative attention, are you now willing to update your Stroke Economy to achieve a better outcome?

SUMMARY

You can manage your children's behaviour most effectively if you give plenty of positive attention to build up their self-esteem, allow them age-appropriate responsibility for their own actions and learning, and limit negative attention. Children need to be loved in ways that feel good to them, but they also need to learn that undesirable behaviours lead to isolation and negative consequences. You can improve your self-esteem by rejecting inappropriate negative strokes and setting up to get more positive attention.

Chapter 11

Managing Power Struggles

Have your children's power struggles driven you up the wall? Here are some useful tactics to help you all enjoy being separate individuals in a supportive unit.

What do you mean?

Take a simple sentence like, 'Right, I'll make dinner then.' When you read it, it seems perfectly cheerful and unambiguous. But how would you say it if you were resentful or depressed, or if you wanted the other person to feel guilty? Much of communication doesn't go on at the surface, social level. It happens at the psychological level. That's what people respond to far more than to words. Even making statements in a flat tone carries information about how the speaker feels.

In addition, the person hearing the message will be in a particular frame of mind, which means that how they interpret the message can be distorted. Children who've spent all day at school being told what to do may answer a straightforward request like 'Will you lay the table please?' with a bad-tempered 'You're always nagging!' or a whiny 'Can't I ever have five minutes' peace and quiet?'

What happens next depends on the psychological positions of the parent and child. The parent might respond bossily, angrily, aggressively or resentfully, or with emotional blackmail or a resigned, 'Oh, never mind, I'll do it.' Or, of course, they may provide a calm but firm repetition of the request, perhaps adding, 'I'm sorry you're tired, but you can have your peace and quiet after that.' Which of these choices is likely to invite the child into compliance, and which into arguments and overt or suppressed rebellion?

Christine, a single mother locked into a cycle of arguments with fifteen-year-old daughter **Lucy**, was unhappily discovering this. She'd wanted Lucy to come to therapy too, but Lucy was having none of it. Christine told me, 'Lucy's impossible. She's an argumentative little madam. Children ought to do as they're told, but she just answers back and flounces out. She's going right off the rails and with her exams coming up I'm worried to death about her. I love her but don't like her at all. I just can't get through to her.'

A lot of parents will know just how Christine felt. If, like her, you want to find ways of managing your interactions with your family, so you all have a better chance of feeling good about yourselves, this next section could hold the answers.

Communication styles

You can divide communication into five styles. These are Controlling Parent, Nurturing Parent, Adult, Adapted Child and Free Child.

- **Controlling Parent** can be both good and bad. 'Don't run into the road!' has a positive intention for the listener. If a teacher yells, 'You're useless! You never do anything right!' he's acting as a negative Controlling Parent. He might have a positive intention for the listener but he's discounting her validity as a person. That's damaging and counter-productive.
- **Nurturing Parent**, oddly enough, can also be good and bad. Showing sympathy and love, having good times with your child and helping him learn are all positive aspects of nurturing. They show you value and respect him. Negative Nurturing Parent behaviours discount the other's abilities. Examples include baby Fred's mother whose smothering love meant Fred didn't need to speak (*see page 74*), and the father who made all his grown-up son's decisions for him, sending the message that he regarded his son as inadequate.
- **Adult** communication is using all your skills and abilities to

respond to the current situation. Even small children have their own age-appropriate Adult ways of functioning. There's no downside to this.

- **Adapted Child** behaviours have good and bad aspects too. When you were little you learned these behaviours to help you adapt to fit in with the adults around you. The positive sides help you get your needs met with the minimum of trouble. Saying 'please' is likely to get you what you want without alienating other people. Negative Adapted Child behaviours, though, discount your adult resources. Some people learned as children that they were most acceptable to their parents when they showed happiness rather than anger, fear, pain or sadness. One woman was so stuck in Adapted Child mode that even when she was rushed into hospital with an agonising ruptured appendix she was still smiling. If only she'd allowed herself to feel her pain she could have been diagnosed earlier and saved herself a lot of suffering. Adapted Child behaviours include sulking and the two-edged satisfaction of being rebellious to 'show' other people. They seldom get you what you want or allow you to feel good about yourself.

- **Free Child** behaviours are uncensored. You cry if you're sad and yell if you're angry. You can do things just for fun. Only if your uncensored behaviour is dangerous or disrespectful is there a negative side to it.

You'll notice that I've spoken sometimes of behaviour and at other times of communication. That's because if other people are present, behaviour is also a way of communicating. If someone is speaking to you and you turn your back, that conveys your desire not to talk to them. How did this solve Christine and Lucy's communication problems, and how can it solve yours?

Inviting positive responses

I asked Christine to draw a chart showing how much of her time with Lucy she spent in each of the communication styles. This is known as an Egogram. Here's what she drew.

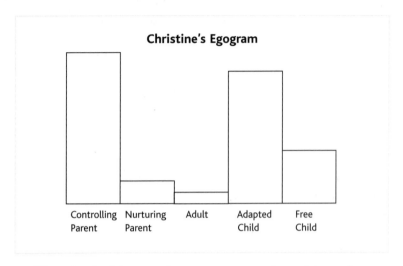

Christine's Egogram

| Controlling Parent | Nurturing Parent | Adult | Adapted Child | Free Child |

Then I asked her to draw a representation of how she saw Lucy's behaviours.

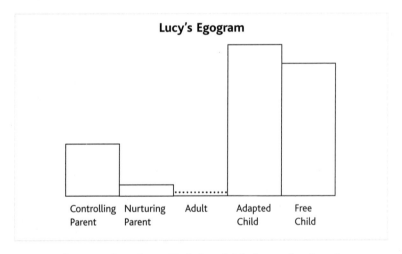

Lucy's Egogram

| Controlling Parent | Nurturing Parent | Adult | Adapted Child | Free Child |

In other words, when Christine laid down the law Lucy was equally bossy or outright rebellious. When Christine lost her temper, Lucy did the same. Sometimes Christine wept or pulled her own hair out, calling herself a bad parent. Then Lucy would usually cry or smash her own possessions. Sometimes she hugged her mother or made her a cup of tea. In Adapted Child mode Christine felt dependent on Lucy's good opinion of her so she'd try to buy

Lucy's affection with treats she couldn't afford. You'll notice that Christine didn't recognise any Adult behaviour in Lucy at all. When I asked her to think about whether this was the case, she went back and put in some Adult, which I've represented with a dotted line.

As Christine had done her best, trying the same strategies, only harder, when she couldn't impose her will, I invited her to relax and do something different. It was only the realisation that what she'd been doing hadn't worked that led her to agree.

You only have so much emotional energy at any one time, so instead of putting so much into Controlling Parent, why not shift some of it into another area? Christine thought Nurturing Parent and Adult would help. Also, because Christine hadn't had much fun lately, she could invest in the pleasant side of Free Child. She then chose some ways of interacting with Lucy that would show these decisions. They were:

Nurturing Parent
Listening sympathetically to Lucy relating problems at school but not offering help unless Lucy asked for it; praising Lucy when possible; hugging her when she would accept this; telling her when she looked pretty; sitting on the side of the bed entertaining her before saying goodnight.

Adult
Recognising that Lucy was a separate individual responsible for her own moods, thinking and actions; that she was almost a grown woman with capabilities of her own; that she was good at getting what she wanted so she was likely to be able to look after herself and that she was working well at subjects she liked. Rather than laying down the law she could ask Lucy in an adult way to consider consequences and self-protection. To strengthen her grasp on her own Adult aspect Christine would list her own good points, valuing past and present good times with her daughter. As Lucy's father had had a big impact on Lucy's behaviour, Christine didn't need to take all the blame. To help Christine stay in Adult rather than Adapted Child, she wouldn't invite Lucy to support her emotionally, which blurred the boundaries of their

mother-daughter relationship and felt burdensome to Lucy. Christine would discuss her problems with her friends instead.

Free Child

Christine deserved some fun. She could relax with some of the TV programmes Lucy enjoyed and her own favourites. Rather than expecting Lucy to meet all her social needs, Christine could contact friends for evenings out.

I didn't see Christine for a fortnight. When she came back she said, 'It's amazing! We're getting on much better. I enjoy being around Lucy a lot more than I did. She's a bit mellower because I'm supportive rather than critical. We've still had some arguments but they're not as ferocious. I feel much better about myself as a parent.'

Christine continued to share more positive interactions so Lucy stopped tuning her out. Christine didn't always find it easy to stop her old habit of critical labelling, but she was learning. She forgave herself when she slipped. Lucy was learning assertive behaviours by example and sometimes even consulted her mother. Being treated more as an adult helped her develop as one. Are you willing to try another style of communicating with your family?

Clear communication

Christine found another tactic useful, too. She'd been apprehensive about how Lucy might react to criticism, so often phrased negative comments obliquely. For example, she'd made statements like, 'Someone around here needs to hang their coat up,' or 'Intelligent people do their homework.' Both of these statements contain criticism at a psychological level, so Lucy had felt attacked and had therefore chosen not to respond or had been hostile rather than cooperative. Because such statements blur the *I-You* boundaries, they discount the separateness of speaker and listener too.

Christine started to use the Emotional Literacy formula you've already come across (*see page 35*) and phrased requests like this: 'When you leave your coat on the sofa I feel annoyed. Please will you hang it up when you come in?' Since the boundaries between Christine and Lucy were now clearer, Christine could recognise what she was accountable for, and what Lucy was. Now Christine didn't have to worry so much. Once she'd said it, the choice was Lucy's. This helped Lucy feel more adult and so encouraged compliance.

To maintain the boundaries Christine often had to bite her tongue as nagging only brewed an adversarial attitude and didn't get things done. But Lucy was the one who could either hang her coat up or not, do her homework or not. As it happened Lucy liked her coat, so if Christine laid it behind the sofa Lucy felt irritated. She therefore chose to hang it up much more often. She was still rather slapdash and sporadic with her homework, but Christine recognised this as Lucy's choice and Lucy as the one who would bear the consequences. As a good parent Christine had pointed these out. Now she left it up to Lucy. Come August Lucy's own disappointment with her results stimulated her into working harder and organising a retake of her maths exams, knowing (because her teachers had told her) that if she didn't pass them, she'd find it harder to get into university.

Since Christine had stopped taking on so many of her daughter's responsibilities, Lucy recognised them as her own and was much more likely to engage with them out of self-interest. By taking a step back and allowing herself and her daughter to be separate, Christine had got more of what she wanted.

Choices in attribution

Psychologically speaking, attribution means describing someone to another person. Previously, as a manipulative shaming tactic, Christine had formed the habit of telling Lucy's relatives and friends in front of her daughter, 'Talking to Lucy's like banging your head against a brick wall.' There were multiple intentions behind this: to shame Lucy into changing her ways by labelling her negatively; to invite other people to criticise Lucy so she'd do something different; to let Christine avoid taking responsibility for attitudes she believed were common so Lucy wouldn't blame her mother; and finally Christine hoped to avoid Lucy's hostile reaction by speaking in public.

The result, however, had been embarrassment for Lucy and everyone else, and generally as soon as the others had gone Lucy would have a slanging match with her mother. Besides, global statements like these don't indicate specific behavioural changes you'd like to see. As they attack the child's self-esteem rather than the unwanted behaviour, they're likely to invite bad feelings and rebellion.

Christine now decided that she would praise Lucy in public. This sent positive messages to and about her daughter, so Lucy's self-esteem was supported. Although Lucy's grandmother was likely to discount positives and dwell on the negatives, Christine now started to stick up for her daughter thereby building up greater solidarity with her. Other people were also glad not to be embroiled in family squabbles and admired the new, more confident Lucy. What about you – if you want to make things better at home, are you willing to use clear, direct communication?

SUMMARY

If you change your own behaviour your children (and others!) will usually come to respond to you differently. By emphasising the positives in your child and allowing her age-appropriate personal responsibility, you're likely to improve your relationship, earn more respect and engender more self-respect in her. When you stop carrying the full weight of your developing child's life (while maintaining suitable care and safety) you'll have more energy to make the best of your own life.

Chapter 12

Updating Your View of Yourself and the World

If you've been thinking you're a terrible parent with awful children, updating your perspective could make life easier all around.

Where did I go wrong?

When your children are being difficult it's hard not to blame yourself. Lots of parents say, 'Where did I go wrong?' if their child misbehaves. One of them was **Liz**, who was extremely distressed when her nine-year-old son **Darren** was diagnosed with Attention Deficit and Hyperactivity Disorder (ADHD). She thought she should have brought him up better, a state of mind which wasn't helped by her husband **Luke** repeating, 'Your son's such a pain because you're useless as a mother.' Between guilt, the stress of managing a demanding child and her husband threatening to leave if she didn't do something about 'that child', she thought she was the worst mother ever. Luke refused to come to therapy because he said their problems were all her fault.

Liz needed both a way to feel better about herself as a parent and some tactics for helping her son learn more acceptable behaviour. There'll be more about behaviour management in this and later chapters, but first let's see whether Liz needed to blame herself. If she didn't, how could she stop? Could she develop a more positive perspective instead? What about you? Would a more positive view help you solve problems, too?

Reality checking

Although people usually think they're responding to reality, in fact humans react to their own interpretation of it. You've only to listen to two people arguing to discover that. Phobias offer further proof of the way people react to their take on reality. To one person, that harmless spider scuttling across the carpet is a terrifying threat that obliterates all other concerns. To others it is just a little creature you can happily pick up in your hands. How, then, can you check your reality? Here are some suggestions.

Replace emotional interpretation with reason

Liz felt like a bad parent so she thought she was one. Feeling and thinking, though, are two different things, and it's important to separate them out. Feelings aren't facts. Everyone can agree on a fact because you can look it up in a reference book. The more you base your thinking on facts instead of feelings the easier life gets. Liz knew she loved Darren despite his troublesome behaviour. In therapy she recognised that she'd kept her adventurous son safe and healthy; that he loved her and often showed it; that there was a lot about him that was lovable; that he had many excellent qualities and skills; and that her five-year-old daughter **Heather** was well behaved. Liz *is* a good parent, and was so relieved when she recognised this that she cried.

Replace elasticated time with real time

Liz had renewed her upset each time people told her of Darren's disruptive behaviour. She said, 'Darren's *always* been a handful. *Whenever* I have friends round he's *constantly* interrupting. He *always* wakes up early so I'm *constantly* tired. When he was five and Heather was a baby he gave her a bath at four in the morning. It was water pouring down the stairs that woke us up. Luke went bananas because Darren could have drowned her. Darren was screaming that he was only being helpful and he'd taken good care of Heather. He's never done it again but we're *always* on edge wondering what he might be up to in the night, so we're *always* shattered. I worry *constantly* what he's going to be like when he's full grown.'

I acknowledged that Darren did have an ongoing problem so her anxiety was understandable. However, I challenged words like *always, constantly* and *never*, which served to keep Liz anxious even when she didn't need to be. She could replace them with *sometimes* and *one day*.

Darren did good things, too. He was bright and had quickly learned to read and write (and to not give his baby sister midnight baths!), which meant he could learn other things as well, such as how to behave more acceptably. He could concentrate on computer games and was starting to transfer this concentration to lessons he enjoyed. I reassured her that adults with ADHD could hold down good jobs, particularly in creative fields, and that as Darren loved his mother and Heather he'd be able to form other loving relationships. While Darren was at school she could let go of worry because his teachers were responsible for him. As Liz worked from home she could catch up on her sleep after lunch. At first Liz hid this 'guilty secret' from her critical husband, but being less tired resulted in increased productivity. Her more relaxed attitude helped Darren feel acceptable so he didn't need so much attention.

By holding herself stuck in *never* and *always*, Liz had discounted the possibilities of change. Altering his diet helped Darren calm down, although medication didn't. Liz could adapt her tactics so Darren got more attention for good behaviour. By centring herself in the *now* Liz realised that bad things would pass, so her anxiety lessened. She had more strength to deal with current difficulties and found greater pleasure in doing enjoyable things.

Replace mind reading with facts

Every time Liz saw Darren's teacher she'd felt guilty because she'd assumed the teacher was thinking, 'She's a bad parent.' Actually the teacher was well aware that Liz was doing her best in a situation that would be hard for anyone. It was only when the teacher saw Liz crying that she acknowledged this sympathetically. For Liz it was as though someone had shone a light in a dark place.

Realising that she wasn't universally condemned, Liz bravely asked her friends what they thought of her parenting skills and discovered they saw a lot of good in the way she related to her children. Eventually, she asked Luke too if he saw any good in her and was moved to tears when he said, 'Of course I do! I love you, don't I?' He also acknowledged that she had far more patience with Darren than he did.

Use your crystal ball positively

All of us store dreads as half-glimpsed pictures that seem to represent the entire future. These reinforce the dreads and prolong anxiety states. Liz had nightmare visions of Darren in jail or homeless on the streets, so she'd become increasingly punitive and Darren had rebelled. Instead of worrying about Darren's whole future all at once Liz began to imagine positive outcomes, seeing him getting good results in his favourite subjects, having a nice girlfriend and a good job. Her new optimism meant she became less critical and more positive towards him. He in turn grew less rebellious and developed greater self-esteem as he found it easier to earn positive attention.

Don't magnify negatives

Liz's focus on the negative things about Darren meant she'd discounted his good points. The more she recognised these, the easier their relationship became.

Value the good

The more praise Liz could legitimately give Darren, the greater became his confidence and the less his need for negative attention. Patient Heather, waiting in the shadows, also felt more secure as Liz could now give her more affection without feeling guilty about favouritism. Luke noticed the improved atmosphere at home and found to his surprise that he could recognise good qualities in his son, so the father-son relationship grew less strained. Heather began to feel less selfish about getting praise from her father.

Reject misidentification

Previously both Liz and Luke had labelled Darren naughty, self-centred and so on. Naturally the boy had decided he was all these negative things. When Liz, and later Luke, began to label the behaviour and not the child, Darren realised he wasn't unacceptable. It was just certain of his behaviours that his parents disliked. By avoiding these he could feel more valued. Instead of saying, 'You're a naughty boy!' they began to say, 'Darren, drawing on the walls is naughty. Please draw on drawing paper instead.' He now had clear guidelines for what would get him into trouble and what wouldn't, so it was easier for him to be good. Likewise Liz stopped calling herself a bad mother, recognised her good points and accepted that there were things she could usefully change. What parent couldn't say the same?

Turn obligation into choice

Liz had been telling herself, 'I *should* be a better mother.' This all-encompassing criticism refreshed her low opinion of herself. Now she started saying, 'I'm a good mother but I *could* . . .' For example, she *could* find positives in Darren and she *could* give more attention to Heather when Darren occupied himself. Replacing words like *should* and *must* with *could* leaves you with choices so you feel more in control.

Widen your focus

Liz realised her image of herself had come to be centred around Darren's naughty actions and her consequent feelings of inadequacy. Valuing herself *only* if her son behaved well at all times meant she couldn't value herself at all. This blinkered attitude had stopped her seeing any of the positive things about herself, like being a good cook, contributing to the household income, being attractive and having friends who liked her very much. Instead of concentrating on her husband's blameful attitude she could take account of his sporadic affection and sympathy so she felt more secure and less as though she had to be perfect to keep him.

Replace extremism with perspective

Both Liz and Luke had been using an extreme perspective. They had seen Darren as *absolutely awful* and themselves as *completely inadequate*. The psychological purpose of extremism is to help you focus on the problem so you can find a solution, but if the problem is long term, extremism is counter-productive because it promotes 'stuck' feelings of anxiety and helplessness. Replacing extremism with a more balanced view let both Liz and Darren feel more lovable and secure.

Put borders around responsibility

It's not uncommon for people, particularly parents, to feel responsible for everything their family does. To an extent it's true that parents *are* responsible for their children's behaviour. If your daughter puts a ball through someone's window, it's up to you to make sure the window is replaced. Liz, though, now realised she wasn't responsible for her son's condition or Luke's intolerance. She could choose her own thoughts, feelings and actions. Luke too had an input in parenting.

As things improved Luke confessed to Liz that he'd been blaming her because he felt helpless about Darren's naughtiness. While parents are responsible for their children's emotional and physical well-being, successful child development is about the child progressively accepting responsibility for his own actions and their consequences.

The Results

Slowly Darren's behaviour improved. Although he still had problems with some teachers, his overall performance was better. He could channel energy into sports where he won awards. His self-esteem grew and, as he felt more valued and secure, he acted up much less than he had done. His sister blossomed as she felt more important and better about herself. Tensions within the family relaxed and the atmosphere at home was much warmer and more accepting all around.

Liz grew confident and optimistic, enjoying the love of her children and the support of her friends. Luke came to see that he wouldn't get the loving relationship he wanted with his wife unless he changed the way he related to her. Although he never did come to therapy he couldn't continue to treat his wife the same way since she'd changed. Now their family is generally much happier. You too can use these counters to thought distortions; to recap, they are:

- Replace emotional interpretation with reason.
- Replace elasticated time with real time.
- Replace mind reading with facts.
- Use your crystal ball positively.

- Don't magnify negatives.
- Value the good.
- Reject misidentification.
- Turn obligation into choice.
- Widen your focus.
- Replace extremism with perspective.
- Put borders around responsibility.

SUMMARY

Separating out feeling from fact helps you develop a healthier and more realistic perspective. You can value the good things and tackle problems from a position of greater strength, which builds confidence and optimism. By teaching your children these skills you can help them find more effective strategies for managing their difficulties, too.

Chapter 13

Minimising Friction by Addressing Your Positive Payoff

When you and your family have had a hard time communicating without friction, identifying positive payoffs can help you all to feel heard and understood.

Negative payoffs

In discussions with your family have you ever had a painful awareness that goes, 'Huh? How did we end up with these horrible feelings again?' You know the sort of thing: you tell your young daughter she can't go to an all-night rave and before you know it you're in the middle of a massive row. What starts as a caring safety message gets transformed into your child being labelled thoughtless and irresponsible while you find yourself being called the parent from hell.

Whatever the subject you're discussing, if you recognise familiar bad feelings at the end of it, what you're getting is a negative payoff where you'd hoped for a positive one, in this case that your child would act responsibly for her own good and perhaps even acknowledge your loving intentions. If you recognise a pattern of repetitive bad feelings with your own family, you may have tried to put the negative payoff behind you and forget about it. Unfortunately if you blank the negative payoff, you run the risk of unconsciously inviting similar results again and again by using the same approach.

Sometimes, then, you have to look not at what you'd hoped to achieve but at what you actually keep getting. Once you let yourself take notice of the bad feelings, that is, the negative payoff, you'll start realising that you need to do something different if you want to invite a positive payoff instead. Since it's always easier to spot someone else's blind spots, here's the story of single mother **Nita,** her teenage son **John** and her boyfriend **Kevin.** As you read it, see if you can identify the negative payoffs her behaviour has been inviting. Do you have repeating negative payoffs of your own that you'd like to replace with positive ones?

You never listen to me!

'How would you like it if your teenager screamed, "You never listen to me!" right in your face?' It was obvious how Nita felt: agitated and aggressive. Her arguments with her fifteen-year-old son John sometimes ended in fights and she was enraged, blameful and scared. In the same situation I've seen other parents sag with feelings of hurt and negation, or on fire with a sense of injustice. Still others are just baffled. Meanwhile the child generally feels upset and thinks there's something wrong with him for 'making' his parents feel bad.

I imagine that at least half of all parents sometimes find themselves on the receiving end of similar accusations from their teens. The ones who don't get this are very lucky, extraordinarily good parents or so repressive that their children are too scared to offer even the mildest of criticisms, which doesn't bode well for their future. Or, of course, the parents and children are so enmeshed that independent thought isn't on the cards.

The fact is, though, that teenagers have to separate out from their parents. The task of adolescence is to become an individual in your own right. This isn't easy, although adults tend to forget just what a struggle it can be.

Here's why it's so hard. Before birth babies are literally part of their parents. In infancy they're dependent for nourishment, safety and well-being. The mother's mood is bound up with the child's and vice versa. The child offers chances to play (a pleasure the mother may have forgotten) and the mother supplies the adult thinking and actions that the child can't manage for himself. In some senses they function as a single unit. Mother and child form part of each other's environment, along with any other close relatives. As the child grows he will meet outside influences such as school and friends, but the centre of his world will still be his mother.

In adolescence the child becomes increasingly aware that one day he'll have to spread his wings and fly the nest. He begins to compete with peers for his place in the social pecking order. At the same time the hormonal seas of puberty bring changes in his body and can carry the teenager away on tides of confusing new emotions. Lacking experience and maturity, he has to cope with all these demands using limited skills of thinking, feeling and behaviour.

All these changes are liberating but they can also be scary. However much the teenager longs for independence he can still get into scrapes from which he needs rescuing. However much he kicks against parental limits he still sometimes wants the shelter of home. He's developing an awareness that unlike cartoons the real world isn't an effortless 'happy ever after'. Having to handle all the practicalities of adult life can seem overwhelming. Nevertheless, adulthood beckons with its exciting possibilities. For a while he's likely to oscillate between grown-up and childish attitudes. He still has to break through the confines of the old parental bond and the fear of leaving childhood security behind. What helps him make this huge life-change is anger. Teenage anger is largely developmental rather than personal – although it's hard to remember that when you're the one your child is yelling at! Below are some ways of promoting harmony.

Repeating cycles of arguments

Though they had rows and even fights, Nita wasn't a bad mother or John a bad son. They loved each other and spent pleasant times together. They talked reasonably freely and offered mutual support. Sometimes, as in most families, one would take out their bad mood on the other, but the rows tended to be short-lived and end in apologies and hugs. Generally, the intentions behind their disagreements were positive. Nita wanted John to take responsibility for his own education, well-being and safety, and to do his fair share of chores. John on his part wanted more freedom, and to make sure that his mother would be happy with her new partner. On a less conscious level he was trying to separate out as an individual.

Their more explosive rows, though, had serious negative payoffs. Because the rows became not about reaching an agreement but about point scoring, Nita and John both felt disrespected and hurt. Each doubted their own worth and lovableness. Both of them felt too ashamed to talk about their arguments to friends or family. Sullen resentments would smoulder for days. The more Nita came over as the heavy parent, the more John responded as the rebellious child.

What they needed was to achieve the positive payoffs they wanted. In outline these were that John would become more trustworthy and responsible; that he and his mother could learn to accept their differences but still love each other; and that mother and son could develop their own confidence and independence while maintaining contact. Don't forget that as the child separates out, so must the mother. Having spent over a decade as part of a mother-child unit, it's hard for her to let go too.

Once you've identified the positive payoffs, the next question is how to attain them. How could Nita manage her son's rages without getting into a fury of her own? And what of you? What negative payoffs do you want to replace with positive ones, and how can you do this?

Feeling, thinking and behaving

There are three ways of responding to an event: feeling, thinking and behaving. Everyone has their own preferred first channel. Nita's way of responding to actions she disliked was to try and stay calm by thinking logically. She believed that thinking was adult and hoped to avoid arguments this way. But denying her feelings didn't mean they didn't exist. Keeping a lid on her anger just built up the pressure until she exploded.

John did the same. After all, he'd learned his style of arguing from her. Nita's fiancé **Kevin** used the same tactics with the same results. Sooner or later one of them would crack and fly into a rage. When Nita and John came to blows, Kevin pulled them apart so John lashed out at him too. These negative payoffs were threatening the existence of the relationship Nita and Kevin wanted, so the situation seemed desperate. In later chapters there's more about step-families, but for now let's stick to achieving positive payoffs.

Feelings are where we're most alive. If you block your feelings channel to avoid painful emotions, you'll also restrict good feelings from getting through. If a child pretends he doesn't have painful feelings he doesn't learn how to manage them. As a child Nita hadn't been allowed to show anger so she didn't know how to deal constructively with it either. That was why she believed feelings weren't adult.

An additional problem is that if you get stuck in one of the channels – feelings, thinking or behaving – you won't necessarily have access to the others at that time. Try telling someone who's hysterical to reason out the situation and you'll see what I mean. The person's not being deliberately obstructive. It's just that if you're locked into one channel it's hard to tune in to the others. Yet you need all three to resolve difficulties because all three offer information you need *and* possible solutions.

Nita now learned that it's adult to respond to here-and-now situations with all your resources, including feelings. Being aware that something hurts means you can think about what to do to solve the problem.

Having discovered that there are degrees of anger and that some of them are legitimate and safe, Nita's next task was to recognise how she felt. This was hard as she'd had a lifetime's training in not acknowledging uncomfortable feelings, but she got there one step at a time. Her way into feelings was to think about them. All this helped her apply the Emotional Literacy formula discussed in Chapter 3. For example, she said, 'I'm worried when I don't see you doing your homework. Please will you show me that you're taking responsibility for it?'

Her next task was to learn to recognise John's feelings, which also meant helping him identify them. As his mother she'd tended to mind-read his emotions, but sometimes she got it wrong. This was one point where he'd retort with, 'You never listen to me!' She was sad and somewhat scared because not knowing what was going on for him threatened the old mother-child bond.

In the past she'd covered up for feeling hurt by retaliating. As many mothers do, she took on the same emotions as her child. This was an enactment of her family's destructive belief that if you love someone you have to feel the same as he does.

There was one feeling Nita hadn't accept from her son. The rules in her family of origin said, 'Males mustn't be scared', so if John had expressed fear she'd responded with, 'Don't be such a baby! Of course you're not!' Now, though, she acknowledged his feeling but didn't have to share it. She might say, 'You're looking worried. Are you?' and was sympathetic if it was appropriate. Since part of the task of any emotion is to communicate, John now knew his feelings were validated. He no longer needed aggression to hammer the point home. As the emotion had done its job he could access his thinking and decide what to do. He and his mother could set about addressing what they wanted changed.

You'll realise that this underpins the 'ERO' technique discussed in Chapter 3. There are three steps involved in this. These are:

- **Empathise**, that is, acknowledge the other person's feeling.
- **Reflect**, which means check out what the feeling is and why it's there.
- **Own**, which means recognise that only your feelings, thinking and actions are your own. The other person's belong to them, not you.

A helpful spin-off from using this technique is that you help your child to separate out emotionally from you in a positive way, so he doesn't need so much anger to break into independence. With practice you'll find it easier and there'll be fewer rows. Those you do have are likely to be less damaging.

The Results

Now Nita had identified the negative payoffs and the positive ones she wanted instead, we rehearsed ways in which she might negotiate with John to bring down used crockery from his room before it turned into a biology project. I was eager to hear how they'd got on with this but she began the next session by saying, 'The first thing I did when I went home last week was ask John what he felt about my coming to therapy. He was a bit cagey at first. It turned out that he thought I was just coming to tell you how horrible he was and he was scared you'd say everything was his fault. I reassured him I was coming mostly for myself but that if I could learn ways of getting on better with him it would be good for both of us.'

She went on, 'He agreed but was still wary. Then I told him I felt hurt when he said I never listened to him, and asked him why he thought that. He said, "Because half the time you're working. You don't look at me and you're miles away." I'd never realised that and I apologised. Now he gets my attention by saying "Mum" and doesn't go on until I look at him.'

So how had she got on with the dirty crockery? 'Fine, actually. He'd just said it was great being treated like an adult so I said, "You know when you don't bring your cups down I get cross because they go smelly? Will you remember to bring them down with you?" and he said, "Sure, if it means that much to you." Now he usually does bring them down, and I say thank you, so that's one thing we don't row about any more. We've had a few niggles, but mostly it's been good. Now I'm listening to his feelings without telling him off for having them, he's talking to me more too.'

SUMMARY

If you recognise the negative payoffs from your style of handling disagreements, you can find more constructive ways of achieving the positive payoffs you want. You can use both feeling and thinking, and own your personal responsibilities and actions. It's helpful to acknowledge the separateness of your and your children's feelings, thinking and behaviour. This will result in them not having to fight so hard to be independent.

Chapter 14

Successful Separation

Has it been hard to help your children deal with separation or divorce? Here are some ways to help them handle the split more comfortably.

Doesn't he love us any more?

This is the terrible cry that rings through souls when families split. Separation and divorce happen to the children too. Sometimes it's the father who keeps the children while the mother moves on. More often, though, it's the father who leaves the family home.

The transition from being a two-parent household to a single-parent one may be relatively smooth. Over a year or two the fallout subsides to a few ripples and the new way of life becomes normal and happy. But sometimes it doesn't. Decades later divorced parents may regret that their children haven't made contact with them in all that time. There are pensioners today whose relationships have been shaped by their responses to their parents' divorce fifty years ago. The outcome depends largely on how such a separation is handled.

I hope you'll never need this chapter. But if you do, here are some ways of giving yourself and your children the best chance of recovery.

You and your children

Leaving a relationship, or being left, is seldom easy. It's not something people do lightly so you'll almost certainly have experienced heartache before or after the decision to leave has been made.

Communication and respect have gone awry somewhere in families that split. I'm not apportioning blame here. It's hard to behave exactly as you'd like when your relationship is crumbling. You'll have lost the closeness and support you'd hoped for, and either one or both partners might lash out in vengeance. You'll be aware you're changing the children's world as well as losing the home you'd built up together. You may be losing daily contact with your children or taking it from the partner you used to love. Indeed, you may still have strong feelings for your ex.

Both adult parties usually feel they're the innocent victim. Even if one or both are moving straight into a longed-for relationship, both probably feel a cocktail of painful emotions like guilt, regret, sadness, anger, jealousy and fear.

At least they're dealing with the separation with a reasonable range of adult skills. Children don't have these resources. Here are ways for parents and children to start dealing with painful emotions. Parent(s) will have to supply what the children need, but this is easier if you're doing as well as you can under the circumstances; before you make any decisions about the children, let's therefore start with relief for adults.

Dealing with loss

If you're going through a separation you have my sympathy. Whether leaver or left, you're trying to deal with a whole new set of practicalities and perhaps support your children's emotions at the same time as coping with your own. These are tough jobs but they can be managed. At first it might be on a 'one day at a time' basis, but little by little you'll move on and find happiness again – if you let yourself.

There's no doubt there are things you have lost: the companionship of that particular partner, the stability and familiarity of that particular set-up, and perhaps (but not inevitably) contact with your partner's relatives and friends. Assuming that you and your partner have been close, you may even feel as though you've lost a part of yourself – but be assured that you haven't. You can help yourself recover more quickly by working out what you have lost and what you haven't.

For almost everyone the pain of loss is a mish-mash of reality and imagination. It's not unusual for a newly separated person to sob, 'He left me so I must be worthless', or 'I'm worthless because I couldn't sustain that relationship'. This isn't true. You still have all the same good qualities and skills you always did. What you've lost is not your worth but your perception of it as mirrored by your ex. The truth is that you are as valuable as anyone else on the planet and you're allowed to know that. Just because one person doesn't want to live with you it doesn't mean no one will. While you might not be feeling at full strength right now, you don't believe your children are worthless if they cry or have flu, do you? The pain of separation is just as valid but of a different nature. You're allowed to feel sad or scared or angry until it passes. Your tears won't dissolve other people.

Another myth is that 'everyone' will be looking at you and will somehow know and condemn you because you're separated. When people feel low they often use emotional reasoning of the type you met in Chapter 12 (*see page 111*): 'I feel worthless so everyone must know I'm worthless.' People who've been in abusive relationships are particularly prone to this fallacy. If they act on it they may avoid contact with friends and family, which is a shame because it cuts them off from support they might receive. Anyone who isn't supportive probably has an axe to grind and you don't have to believe them. You, not they, are the expert on what's been happening for you.

You may believe you've lost the years you spent with that person. You haven't. The good times were there and they were real. Once you've safely used your anger to detach, though, you can let go of bad memories. Even if you enjoy tearing up old photos and love letters, it's a good idea to tuck one of each away so when you're ready you can remember the good feelings you once had. You can also value the helpful lessons you've learned from all this.

Nor have you lost the chance of happiness in the future. Though every instant of every day may seem dark at first, gradually you'll start having bright moments. Eventually these will outnumber the bad times. You can still have fun with the children, go out with friends, enjoy old and new interests and maybe invest in your career. While you may be full of morbid fantasies that your ex is having a wonderful life with someone else, don't forget that he has problems with relationships. How he behaved with you is likely to be how he treats everyone else in a similar role to yours with him.

Just because you're lonely now, there's no need to think you always will be. You can accept friendships and when you're ready you can accept romance again, too, only this time you'll be aware of possible pitfalls and you'll have more experience to help you weed out people you're uncomfortable around and choose partners who'll be good to you. By taking things slowly and using all your feelings you'll have a much better chance of finding good love. As you build up your self-esteem in the ways you saw in the first section you'll not only feel better, you'll also make sure you don't fall into hanging your self-esteem on a rebound relationship just because someone's paying you attention.

The key to a speedy recovery is letting yourself recover. Some people hang on to grief long past its sell-by date, perhaps from an unrealistic belief that they deserve to be punished. Or else they mistakenly believe that if they grieve hard enough their ex will come back and rescue them or just be miserable for the rest of his days. If you've been doing this, you're not the only one. But it doesn't work. You're the one who feels your bad feelings more than anyone else. Once you stop doing this to yourself you open up your chances of finding happiness again. (If your grief is affecting your health, it may be an idea to see your doctor.)

Some fear of the unknown is normal. Beginning life again is a little like sailing into new waters. Just as sailors can avoid reefs by looking at charts, you can feel more certain by plotting the way ahead one step at a time. You're allowed to ask for the information you need from bank managers, lawyers, friends, anyone who could be helpful. Slowly the new situation will become familiar territory and will feel safer and more manageable.

I'm not saying it's comfortable to be unhappy, but it is normal to be sad in sad situations. A good cry lets tears carry grief hormones out of the body. You can treat yourself like an invalid for a few days, curling up with a good book, a hot-water bottle and something comforting like cocoa. You can phone your friends when you're lonely. If you have an attack of midnight desperation you can ring the Samaritans. You can give yourself affordable treats.

You can do things you enjoy even if at first you don't get the same pleasure from them as you normally would. Sensible exercise is useful because it burns off surplus adrenaline so you feel calmer and sleep better. It produces feel-good hormones that help restore your well-being.

It's also normal to feel angry. Just as teenagers need anger to help them separate out from their parents, adults need anger to complete their separation. It is, however, important to use anger intelligently. Revenge just shows the other person what power they had over you. In the long run it's bad for your self-esteem and can also cause you problems with your children or the law.

To use anger safely you have to decide you're not going to hurt yourself or anyone else. Once you've made that decision you could pour out your feelings in a letter to your ex, *which you'll never let anyone see.* It's crucial that your children don't find it. You can put it away for a few days, then rewrite it more calmly. Again hide it away for a while. Finally compose a calm version of the letter, stating briefly and assertively how you feel and what you want. Give it another week before you decide whether or not you're going to send it so you don't do anything you'll regret. Or you could record it on tape.

As long as you're sure you're not going to hurt anyone you might also enjoy drawing a circle with eyes, nose and mouth to represent your ex. You can fasten it to a cushion with elastic bands and derive great release from shouting at it and hitting it. Again, you'll need to make sure that your children can't hear.

Then there's forgiveness. This isn't for the benefit of your ex. It's for you. Holding on to anger is draining. Dwelling on the past means you've less energy to make the best of the present. You might even pity him because he's locked in destructive ways of thinking. If necessary you can practise saying, 'I am now willing to want to forgive X.' It's your call whether or not you forgive him to his face. Inward forgiveness is fine. You can also forgive yourself if you need to. Whatever you did, you acted for the best with the resources you had in those circumstances, and he had choices about how he responded.

People say that recovery takes approximately one month for every year you were together. Counselling or divorce workshops speed your recovery, but the main factor is your willingness to embrace your new life and make it as fulfilling as you can.

Helping your children

Let's go back to, 'Doesn't he love us any more?' Children, with their polarised thinking, find it hard to understand how a parent can leave but still love them. It's even worse if the absent parent cuts contact, which around half of them do. Children commonly fear they're somehow unlovable. Younger ones aren't clearly aware of the difference between themselves and the rest of the world and so may believe it was their fault. Small children may verbalise their fear, while older ones might not because they're afraid of the answer. Or they're afraid to add to the burden of the person who is caring for them. An experience as traumatic as a separation means even teens may regress to a point where they feel they can legitimately expect emotional rescue for a while. Since their centre of stability has been rocked, what they need is lots of extra love and reassurance that things are going to be OK. This lays a foundation of optimism, which gives everyone the best chance of surviving the dark days and working to make things better.

Because the parents are traumatised themselves, they can't always respond as they'd like to. The parent who is the carer is pressurised by extra responsibilities, and if the absent parent has access he may compete for affection with expensive treats. Don't feel you have to compete in return. Love is about understanding, not monetary gain.

You can expect your children to feel sad; guilty; self-conscious and embarrassed; scared they're unlovable; worried about the future; burdened with responsibility for their grieving parent; and hugely angry. I've known previously well-behaved children start insulting their parents, vandalising property or abusing alcohol until they adjust. They may hurt or starve themselves so the parent who is looking after them is terrified. Sometimes parents respond punitively, not least because they're already overburdened. The child feels worse and so acts up even more. This is usually a phase and with support the child soon re-emerges as his normal, pleasant self.

The tasks facing the carer parent are therefore many, but the first one is repeated reassurance – that it's not the child's fault;

that he's still lovable even if you don't like some of his behaviours; that you won't ever abandon the child or stop loving him; and that despite your upset you'll be OK. Life will go on and you'll do your best to make it better for him and for you.

It's a temptation for parents to invite their children to take sides. As you've seen, children are not completely separate though they're in the process of individuation. It's important for parents not to demonise each other. To ask children to be allies against 'the enemy' is to impose a terrible split within them. This is because children know they are carrying parts of both of you. Imagine how destructive it will be for them if they believe that part of themselves is repellent!

If your ex tries to poison your children against you, try not to get upset. As calmly as possible you can encourage them to tell you what he's said. Then you can ask them whether they think it's true. Sadly, there is sometimes a grain of truth in accusations. If necessary you can admit it, apologise and ask them what they think you should do about it. If it's not true you can say, 'I feel quite hurt about that. I don't think it's fair, do you?' Children will in any case make up their own minds in time about whom to trust as they'll see which parent treats them with love, respect and honesty.

Sometimes parents want to continue their power struggle after the separation. Access and custody can be turned into weapons so the children are reduced to pawns in the war. This undermines their self-esteem. Unless the absent parent is likely to abuse or neglect the children, why not let them see him if they want to? This is not only less costly in terms of court cases, but also likely to mean that your children – and you – recover far sooner.

Mediation lawyers can help you arrange periods of access. If possible, frequent, shorter access periods are generally more supportive of children and easier for parents to cope with than longer ones. Regular phone calls and emails are a reasonable substitute in the interim. Unless your children are very young you can avoid arguing with your ex by delivering them to the door and then waiting a short distance away until you've seen them safely inside. Access and child support are separate issues. The bottom line is what's best for the children, and they're the authority on what contact they want.

As you come to manage your emotions you can help your children learn to manage theirs. Children can get release by taking out their anger with a plain pillow (no faces for them) and a table-tennis bat. Parents don't have to pretend they're perfect, unfeeling robots. There's nothing wrong with crying with your children occasionally so long as you're showing them that you're working to make the best of life. It's important that you don't let them believe it's always their job to comfort you. It's yours to take care of them, and to teach them coping skills, not least by example.

To help minimise the children's fear of the unknown it's best to be honest with them. They'll be sensitive to atmospheres, so while you'll no doubt try to be as cheerful as you can they'll know something's wrong. You don't have to tell them absolutely everything (no demonising the ex, remember?) but you can give an edited version. It might be along the lines of, 'Mum and Dad can't live together any more because we have too many rows. It's not because of you; it's us. But we both still love you very much and you're important to us. Dad's moving out so you'll have two homes now. It'll be hard at first but we'll get through all right. Lots of other people do so we're not the only ones and it's OK to talk to your friends about it. Have you got any questions?' If they have any questions you don't know how to answer, you can tell them you'll find out, or you can work it out together. The important thing is that they know they can ask and you'll take them seriously.

SUMMARY

Children as well as parents are hurt by divorce. Being open and respectful of the children's feelings shows you value them. By acknowledging emotions as separate from facts and being willing to let go of your grief and anger, you and your children can help yourselves recover more quickly.

Chapter 15

Supportive Stepfamilies

If blending two families into one has been rocky for you, here are some ways of smoothing the path to harmony.

My partner's son hates me

You may remember from Chapter 13 (*see page 117*) that fifteen-year-old **John** was arguing not only with his mother **Nita,** but also with her boyfriend **Kevin.** Although Kevin and Nita had been intending to live together, John wasn't at all happy about this, sometimes sulking but more often acting rebelliously. Kevin was so put off by the rows that occasionally turned into physical fights that he was having second thoughts. Nita felt torn between them and scared she'd lose one or the other.

John wavered between wanting to drive Kevin away and wanting to keep him around so his mother would be happy. Partly this was expressed around whether or not he'd call the new man Dad or just Kevin. John was also scared his mother thought he was in the way. Sometimes he was anxious that Kevin thought he was in the way too, but sometimes he was glad of it. And at times, if he found himself enjoying Kevin's company, he'd suddenly feel guilty because he wasn't being loyal to his dad.

This is fairly typical of the tensions within stepfamilies. It's not easy dealing with new factors that change existing relationship dynamics but it is possible. Stepfamilies can work extremely well even if they get off to a bit of a rocky start. So how did John, Nita and Kevin settle into a generally happy unit? Could the ideas they used help you too?

What makes me OK?

Starting from an I-U+ Life Position, Kevin had believed he had to control John in order to be an acceptable stepfather and partner. He'd labelled himself 'weak' and 'inadequate' because he didn't know how to stop the arguments.

When the conflicts happened Nita believed she wasn't a good enough mother or partner in Kevin's or John's eyes (I-U+). Meanwhile John too held an I-U+ Life Position since he couldn't prevent Kevin from overpowering him and because his rages were threatening his mother's happiness. Unfortunately for John, he also believed he wasn't good enough because he couldn't protect his mother from Kevin's anger or withdrawal any more than he'd been able to make his alcohol-dependent father behave acceptably or stay in the family.

In other words, each of them believed, 'I'm only good enough if . . .' with a different but unrealistic ending. It wasn't a long step from this to looking for get-out clauses. These were based on premises like, 'I'd be OK if only So-and-So didn't . . .' Let's look at this culture of blame from each person's point of view.

John blamed his mother for setting restrictive parental guidelines that discounted his maturity. He blamed her for her rages and for 'making' him angry. He consciously blamed her for not doing more to make her marriage with his dad work. On a less aware level he blamed her for somehow driving his father away, and for 'making' John himself the kind of person a father would leave. He blamed her for the rare times she'd told him unpleasant truths about his dad. John also blamed her for Kevin's interference in private quarrels between John and his mother.

Nita, meanwhile, blamed John for his teenage moodiness, anger and irresponsible acts. She blamed him for his aggressive arguing techniques, sublimely unaware that he'd copied them for her. She blamed him for spoiling the atmosphere at home and for threatening her happiness by opposing her relationship with Kevin, one she hoped would last after John himself grew up and left home. She blamed him for his resentment towards Kevin and because John interfered when Nita had a disagreement with her boyfriend. Moreover, she blamed John for not being grateful that she'd introduced a nice new stepfather for him.

Kevin's own range of get-out clauses included blaming Nita for not being strict enough with her son and for her ambivalent attitude towards himself. He blamed John for his own feeling of being marginalised and for all the difficulties he was encountering in his unaccustomed parental role. He was angry with John for not automatically calling him Dad. He blamed the pair of them for his own new lack of confidence, which hooked on to self-doubts from his past.

Each of them, outside their conscious awareness, also blamed the others for not fitting in with the accepted but unspoken family rules. They all naturally believed their own set of rules made the most sense. Since each of them had a slightly different set of family rules it would have been well-nigh impossible to prevent this conflict (although they could all learn to handle it better). What it came down to was that each of them felt that they were not good enough in some way and held the others responsible. Rather than resolving the subject of each conflict, they fell into point scoring to feel one-up so the same conflicts arose again and again, with the same positive intentions getting lost in the same negative payoffs. Each person became more entrenched in the belief that his or her own beliefs were right while the other people's were inevitably wrong.

I'm coming to hate words like *right* and *wrong*. Too often people use them to beat themselves up or put other people down rather than to solve problems. Sure, there are moral standards, but I think they're easier to attain while keeping your self-esteem intact if you use words like *helpful* and *unhelpful* instead.

Perhaps this scenario has given you an insight into your own situation. If so, let's see what techniques from this case history you could apply to help your stepfamily blend into a harmonious whole.

Update your thinking

First Nita updated her thinking using the strategies in earlier chapters, especially ERO and Emotional Literacy (*see page 35*). Then she explained them to both John and Kevin in private, leaving them to decide for themselves whether to take these ideas on board. Since she'd already shown she felt better for using them, and since she and John had reached a better understanding using feeling as well as thinking and behaving, Kevin stopped being quite so sceptical. Using a more positive Stroke Economy improved communication and confidence all around.

Each of them also backed off a little. Nita talked things through with them, first separately and then together, emphasising that this wasn't a yes/no, life-or-death situation, but one where they could try it out for a while to see if they could make things work in a way they all liked. If so, great. If not, well, better to find out before they'd committed than after they had done so. Each of them would have further chances for happiness in the future. Kevin would keep his flat but visit at predetermined times, hopefully building up to full commitment.

Kevin, meanwhile, had a new task of his own: to let go of some of his old, rigid, polarised thinking. As a boy he'd seen how his father handled things and had concluded that to earn respect as a parent you had to make your child fear you. Now he discovered that respect and fear are different. For a start, respect isn't damaging or divisive. It's also better for everyone's self-esteem. With respect you acknowledge safe boundaries between each member of the family, allowing everyone their own thoughts, feelings and actions.

Since he no longer attached his self-esteem to forcing John to comply, Kevin lost his sense of weakness. He left the discipline to Nita, respecting her ability to cope with situations and consequences. Of course, if there had been small children around, Kevin might have had to take a more active part in discipline sometimes, giving each child age-appropriate care and respect. Standing back a little didn't mean Kevin no longer cared about them. As things calmed down they all found it easier to enjoy each other's company. The adults started sharing John's favourite TV programmes, accepting his right to like what he liked even if they didn't agree with his tastes. John went fishing with Kevin and found it surprisingly rewarding. It helped them bond, especially as other anglers held Kevin in high regard. Besides, John liked being allowed into the club-house to play snooker.

Now Kevin was behaving more positively towards John, Nita no longer needed to spring to her son's defence. The adults also formed a common policy so John couldn't persuade one of them that the other would permit something unsuitable. They all stopped trying to form shifting alliances against one or another, so the step-family unit became more cohesive. Kevin felt more accepted and secure and so gave them space to enjoy their mother-son bond. Soon Kevin was living more or less full-time at their place.

As you've seen, when one person changes their thinking and behaviour, the others can no longer treat him or her quite the same. Are you willing to update your thinking to get more of what you want?

Respect and family rights

Nita, John and Kevin were increasingly comfortable with each other, but becoming consciously aware of each person's rights was another step forward for them, and one you and your (step)family might find helpful, too.

Each member of the family has the right to feel safe; to make mistakes and still know they're lovable; to make their own age-appropriate decisions and cope with the consequences; to change their minds; and to negotiate for what they want.

You can sum this up with a simple five-point formula for treating yourself and your family with respect. The first letter of each point can be put together to make an easy word to remember: OPERA.

- **Observe** yourself and your family. This gives you information you can act on. Rather than mind reading, labelling or jumping to conclusions you can ask if you're not sure.
- **Pay respect** to your family members. Respect their personal boundaries and the fact that they have positive intentions behind what they do (even if there are sometimes negative consequences!). They may have resources you don't. Since actions speak louder than words they can learn new respectful behaviours from the way you model them.
- **Explain briefly** what you're concerned about and how it's affecting you. Rather than speaking for other family members, leave them to speak up for themselves. 'And another thing!' diatribes alienate or bewilder people, so stick to one point at a time and keep it short.

- **Recognise** that their viewpoint is valid for them and be prepared to compromise.
- **Ask** simply for what you want, realising you might not get all of it.

The Results

Although John still sometimes yo-yo'd between child and adult attitudes, and still needed some anger to help him complete his individuation, the fact that his mother and stepfather showed him a greater degree of respect helped him want to earn it. Now Nita wasn't trying to force him to say Dad, John was able to explain his mixed feelings around the whole concept of a dad because his relationship with his birth father was difficult, so he'd be happier just saying Kevin. Understanding this, Kevin accepted it happily.

In time, each of them felt more secure in their own relationship with themselves and the others. They allowed each other positive attention and space. This isn't to say that everything was perfect. John got really drunk at the first party where he'd been allowed to stay late. Parental repression could once again have invited rebellion and Nita was scared she'd lose her temper, so Kevin offered to handle it using OPERA.

Next day when John had sobered up, Kevin *observed* that John seemed nervous about his mother's possibly punitive response. He *paid respect* to John's intelligence in knowing that nervousness was a reasonable reaction, and again in asking calmly for John's explanation. This blame-free approach aligned them on the same side and encouraged a truthful reply: John hadn't meant to get drunk but had been showing off by drinking a couple of whisky chasers. Now Kevin *explained briefly* the safe approach to alcohol and that Nita and he were worried he might follow his father's alcoholic path. He *paid respect* once more to John's intelligence and *asked* how he'd behave if friends again encouraged him to drink. John said he didn't want to be like his dad, and he'd be more careful. Kevin also *asked* John to apologise to his mother for worrying her.

John could hardly believe that was the end of it, but it was. Once he'd said sorry and given his mother a hug, that was it. He was grateful to his stepfather for being so understanding and was indeed more careful how he drank in the future.

All this has a happy ending, but what if you and your new partner each have children to bring into the mix? How can you help stepsiblings blend more harmoniously?

Stepbrothers and sisters

Children are more likely to compete for their place in the pecking order than to welcome a new brother or sister to share their space, their things and their parent. They'll probably be jealous of each scrap of affection or preferential treatment their stepsibs receive. Already shaken by the loss of one parent's presence, they'll be reluctant to make sacrifices because their belief in their family's stability has been undermined.

In order to feel better about themselves they may want to reinforce their bond with their 'own' caretaking parent. But if their parent is giving attention to the new loving partner the potential for jealousy abounds. Acting on the belief that the newcomer is replacing their own absent parent, children are likely to be resentful of his authority. Children from each side are likely to line up behind their own parent in defiance of the other. Hopeful announcements such as, 'I've found a wonderful new father, sister and brother for you!' are likely to be treated with contempt. Underlying that there is probably fear: if you can replace her father and accept new sons and daughters, are you going to replace her too?

There's one other essential point. Although you may love your son despite his nose-picking and smelly feet, other people may not. Children have a right to their own likes and dislikes and can be outspoken.

It's a good idea to go very slowly and cautiously in the way you introduce your child to what you hope will become her stepfamily. The 'new broom sweeps clean' approach builds hostility. You might first discuss with your own children the idea of your dating. Since most children equate the security of their childhood attachments with their original nuclear family and probably wish Mum and Dad could get back together, they may not be too keen. These feelings will probably be stronger if you deny them access to the absent parent. Besides which, children are usually disgusted to discover their parents are sexual beings.

It may take several months before they're OK about your being out once or twice a week, but they'll be reassured if you're always happy to come home on time to them. Once you're sure you and your partner stand a good chance of sticking together you might introduce him on neutral territory, such as over a burger. Simply calling the new adult by their first name is less likely to lead to conflict than insisting on 'Dad' and 'Mum', which would test their loyalties. Several more relaxed outings spaced out over a couple of months will give him a chance to win some degree of liking and respect. It's a good idea to opt for places the children like, such as theme parks. Beware of shopping precincts and of trying to buy their affection!

Children observe things that a love-blinded parent might not, so you can ask them what they think of him. Take their prejudices seriously and discuss them in the most adult way you can.

If they like him you might start inviting him home from time to time. Once you're all feeling reasonably comfortable about this you could arrange a mass outing with all the children, but one that won't last too long. Again, it's useful to respect their reactions and go slowly in arranging further group meetings.

Since parents are responsible for their children's emotional well-being, it's my view that if any child shows a strong objection over a year or so to the prospective additions to her family, you might put your plans on hold. If she's not being forced into anything, she may gradually accept that blending the two families is a good idea. This will be easier if you discuss with her how it might be done, encouraging her to ask questions and express her anxieties. Hopefully your beloved will be doing the same with his kids. (If he isn't, will he be as welcome a co-parent as you'd hoped?)

If everyone on both sides is in agreement, you could all get together, perhaps at a picnic in a local park. By now everyone should be able to speak freely and respectfully, so you can pool your combined resources. You could ask all the children if blending the two families is what they want and how you can all overcome the difficulties. Everyone should get their turn to be heard. This allows everyone to feel valued so they'll feel safer about coming together. Assuming all parties agree, you might start with a joint weekend away. Getting together on neutral territory will ensure that neither side will feel their space is being invaded until they're used to each other. After that you can gradually spend more time together as a family. Away from the children, you and your partner can agree on how you'll handle discipline, conflict and the division of roles.

SUMMARY
Blending families is easiest if you take things one step at a time. Understanding the fears underlying blame and hostility helps you manage them more supportively. Respecting the children's views may mean putting things on hold, at least for a time. Parents can help themselves by agreeing the family rules in advance. This will help to minimise bickering and power struggles.

Chapter 16

Time and Attention

Have you been feeling martyred and left out? Could you use some ways of reclaiming your life? Here are some ideas.

Where are you?

So far the focus in this section has been on your children. But you too exist as a person with feelings and needs of your own – ones you may have had little energy to fulfil, since you've been supplying a lot of the care for children who can't fend for themselves. As your children develop they'll be less dependent on you unless there's a specific problem. All the same they'll still impose practical and emotional demands on you. Sometimes this is fine but at other times you may reach screaming point!

Antonia felt ready to explode when she came to counselling. She was in her mid-thirties with three children aged between four and fourteen. She said tightly, 'They're sucking the life out of me. My husband **Keith**'s as bad. He works from home so he's always there criticising me. I've always got a headache and a stiff neck. I'm scared I'm going insane.' What Antonia needed was ways of relating to her family while keeping herself safe. The behaviour management ideas you've already met were a big help. But that was mostly about other people. How could she address that empty, used-up feeling inside her? Do you too feel the demands of your family are draining you dry? If so, here are some ways to redress the balance so you can feel better.

Running on 'empty'

Everyone has a blueprint for giving and getting attention. You sketch in the outline for this pattern during the first six or seven years of life and keep repeating it in adulthood. If you were shy as a toddler you'll probably go on to be a shy teenager and a shy adult. Scenes in which you did get positive strokes probably didn't make much impression. You might want to make contact but you'd be frightened of being rejected. If anyone rejected you, you'd be likely to blame yourself. You'd probably interpret many incidents as confirming that being shy is the only possible strategy for you.

That isn't true, though. Your early decisions about yourself in relation to the world were the best tactics you could come up with *at the time*. Back then you didn't have many choices and your thinking skills were limited so, like many others, you may have ended up with seemingly irreversible decisions like, 'I can't speak up for myself' or 'People are horrible to me so it's better if they don't see me.' If you have, you've probably been reluctant to think about giving and getting attention. That means you might be left with those painful decisions

Because things have always seemed that way you probably carry on using the same tactics with the same results, unaware that as an adult you have more options than you had as a child. If you notice other people behaving differently, you probably believe it's because they're them and you can't do things like that because you're you.

In Part I you came across some of the sorts of childhood decisions I'm talking about – decisions like Antonia's I-U+ approach to her family and her belief that she couldn't be OK *until* she'd done everything perfectly for everyone else, which left her feel stuck in some pretty unhappy situations.

When she'd been an accountant, she'd been conscientious but she could stop work at going-home time. As a full-time mother and wife, though, she didn't feel she could put any boundaries in. If the children wanted something, they wanted it *now*. If they left the place in a mess, her home-office husband wanted it tidied up *straight away*. Between family demands and low self-esteem, Antonia didn't feel she could legitimately do anything to get her own needs met. Nor would she admit how she felt because 'they'd only have a go at me'. Day after day from 7 a.m. until midnight she soldiered on, feeling sucked dry. As time went on she felt increasingly ill and blamed herself for that, too.

Because Antonia believed she'd either be engulfed or rejected by her family, she subconsciously tried to put boundaries between them and herself. With her husband this wasn't too hard because he frequently worked fourteen hours a day, though he didn't need to. Because she believed he was observing her critically, she couldn't relax with him but scurried around making the house look perfect. Then he'd criticise her for not doing those tasks before. He felt just as rejected but hid it behind hostility.

With the kids, Antonia found it harder to put safe boundaries in. The little one constantly trailed around after her, asking for stories or games or drinks. Although Antonia gave him what he wanted, emotionally she was miles away. Once he rubbed jam and flour into the new sofa as a plea for attention – but he didn't like the attention he got! He was taking on the Rebel slot.

The oldest lad was off doing teenage things, which was great. He did well at school but seemed rather secretive and aloof. Antonia's anxiety about this was overridden by her relief that he made few demands. He was the Golden Child and she didn't want to see if there might be anything troublesome behind that facade.

Antonia worried most about the middle son. Through no fault of anyone's he was the Pathetic One. He'd been a sickly child and now, aged ten, still had nightmares, although he no longer needed hospitalisation. He fussed every evening to put off going to bed. In the night he'd call out, alarming his little brother who'd also need reassurance.

Antonia acted as a buffer zone between the middle son and his father, whose attitude was 'Stop being such a wimp!' To avoid disturbing her husband Antonia spent hours in the sons' bedroom, often waking cold and cramped from falling asleep on their floor. If her husband caught her he'd tell her off for mollycoddling the boys. Antonia was often too tense to eat. She was underweight, and suffered from irritable bowel syndrome.

It's hardly surprising, then, that Antonia felt drained. It's as though she were some sort of pressure cooker with a lid on it. The lid prevented her from taking in positive strokes but it didn't keep negative ones out. Meanwhile, running almost on empty, she felt the few dregs of energy she had left were always about to blow. She did her best to screw the lid down tight so her sadness,

fear and anger didn't break out. Sometimes she treated herself
to an explosion. Despite some temporary relief, the blow-ups just
earned her isolation or criticism so she soon went back to feeling
empty and hopeless. Meanwhile, she went around with her jaws
clamped to keep back the words she might have spoken. This
accounted for her stiff neck and headaches.

As Antonia wasn't acting on her feelings but on everyone
else's, she sometimes dreamed she was trapped behind a glass
wall, banging and hollering but unable to make anyone notice
her. They were all on the other side of the wall, having a whale
of a time. Then she'd collapse in on herself like a balloon with
a slow puncture.

What Antonia wanted was to learn new strategies that would
get her the attention she needed in ways she could accept. Then
she'd be able to fill herself up and become visible. Does that ring
a bell for you?

Time and attention
There are six ways of getting – or not getting – the attention you
need, ranging from very little attention to true intimacy. You
probably adopted some of these patterns of behaviour to help
you fit into your original family jigsaw. Acting on them confirmed
your early views of yourself as worthy or not worthy because you'll
have invited positive attention, negative attention, or very little
attention at all.

- **Emotional absence** is withdrawing from other people. Married
  to a workaholic (interesting why she chose one, isn't it?), Antonia
  didn't have to work particularly hard at withdrawing from her
  husband. Before the children were born she'd enjoyed solitary
  pursuits like playing the piano, but she had no time for pleasure
  now. When Keith wanted to share attention she feared it would
  be hostile so she did extra chores to avoid that. Meanwhile she
  might be occupied physically with her children's needs while
  being emotionally distant. Sometimes it was pleasant to read in
  the living room while her children did their own thing. That
  was fine. No one felt uncomfortable. It was when she wanted
  to draw back from them that she was emotionally absent. The

younger children felt this loss of connection keenly. They'd chosen the Rebel and Pathetic One options in response. The oldest child had made himself an escape route with his secret life away from home.

- **Recognition** is another way of managing time and attention. The family might pass each other with nothing more than a 'Hi!' Antonia had encouraged this, partly by modelling it and partly because she didn't want to get caught up in a new set of demands. It fitted in well with her husband's preoccupation with business, but didn't help 'fill her up'.

- **Impersonal contact** was one of Antonia's ways of building bridges without opening herself to demands. She and her husband might agree how cold it was now the nights were drawing in or have a desultory discussion about the news. The children might tell their mum about something that had happened at school, but the conversations followed well-worn paths and solved nothing.

- **Parallel contact** implies a contradiction. You're engaged with someone else on a task. Antonia's husband, for example, would mow the lawns while she trimmed the edges. It held some satisfaction. The job got done in a fairly companionable way. But there was no real emotional contact. After all, parallel lines head in the same direction but they never meet.

- **Manipulative contact** is a more powerful way of addressing emotional needs. Both you and anyone you do this with are likely to get intense feelings. However, it works indirectly so it usually backfires. Blame and guilt trips are two of the many forms of manipulative contact.

The middle son had learned that his best chance of getting his mum's attention was by acting ill rather than asking straight out for it. The Rebel used small naughtinesses. The oldest lad didn't play this game because he'd given up. Antonia's frantic efforts to keep the house immaculate and the children quiet were all subconscious pleas for Keith's approval. However, when things were good he didn't notice and her resentment was even greater because he only commented on imperfections. One time she'd spent hours washing the paintwork down. Far from giving her the praise she wanted, her husband said, 'There's mud on the kitchen floor.' For a moment she thought, 'Huh?' and then lost her temper. Her husband was just as baffled because he didn't see why an impersonal remark should provoke a furious outburst.

- **Intimate contact** is an upfront sharing of what you feel. When Antonia's youngest son cried because he'd grazed his knee, his cry was a genuine expression of hurt as well as a direct plea for attention. When his mother kissed him better, put a plaster on the wound and drew a smiling face on it, the boy felt safe and cared for. Antonia felt good too when he spontaneously threw his arms around her neck and said, 'I love you, Mummy!' Intimate contact isn't always pleasant. Keith's real anger when one son accidentally scratched the new car was a true expression of his feelings. When he said he was scared that Antonia was ill, that was intimate. But Antonia smiled and pretended she was OK to win approval. That was a manipulation.

Intimacy carries a perception of risk. The fear is that if you show what you're really feeling, the other person can hurt you. Antonia didn't want to know her husband was concerned about her. She thought his fear would stop him supporting the family, and believed her illness invited him to despise her or leave her for being weak. Her fake smile was a request for him to go back to taking her for granted. She didn't want to be responsible for his feeling upset.

The risk isn't authentic, though, because it implies a discount of either you or the other person. Even if she'd died Keith would have managed to bring up the children. The same for her if he wasn't around. Keith was responsible for how he felt, not her. He could carry on working while he was worried. After all, she did!

Managing time to get the attention you need

Antonia's positive intention for her hiding behind *emotional absence, recognition, impersonal contact* and *parallel contact* was to prevent herself from being drained by her family. What she'd actually got was to feel lonely and disregarded. By investing in *manipulative contact* she'd invited bad feelings rather than the warmth and love she craved.

Once Antonia realised she'd been setting herself up to keep on feeling empty and invisible, she followed a common way of getting the kinds of strokes she was used to: she blamed herself and felt terrible. She didn't need to. It wasn't as though she'd been doing it on purpose. All this had been going on beneath her conscious awareness. It was a pattern she'd copied from her family of origin and it had got her through this far. Her children were healthy and well cared for, and she and her husband loved each other in their own way.

Now, though, Antonia had the chance to start doing something different. She could take the decision to recognise her own feelings and act on them. This reinforced her new decision that she was acceptable.

Putting more emotional attention on the children, Antonia got more back so she felt *less* isolated. After a period of shock and adjustment her eldest son came to regard her as a real person instead of a robot. Her other sons didn't need to be naughty or ill to claim her attention, so Antonia's contact with them became more rewarding. Gradually she was allowing her emptiness to fill up.

Meanwhile she could give herself some positive attention as well. A massage from a physiotherapist loosened her neck muscles somewhat. While the little one was at nursery she took relaxation classes or played the piano. All this, combined with no longer having to clamp her jaw to hold in painful emotions, meant she felt better physically. She regained some appetite and although she's still underweight she no longer suffers so badly from an irritable bowel.

Next Antonia needed to tackle her husband. It took time to work up the nerve to ask him if he sometimes felt isolated. It was as though a dam had burst. He began to speak of what was going on for him. She opened up a bit too, and when nothing nasty happened she spoke more freely. They now make time for each other.

As Antonia says, 'It's not perfect but it's a hell of a lot better. I feel like a human being instead of an automaton. When I get upset, I ask myself whether I'm getting the attention I need. Now I know if I'm feeling unheard or invisible it's my job to make my presence felt.'

SUMMARY

If you've been scared that you would be engulfed or rejected, you'll probably have felt lonely and unhappy too. By working out positive ways of spending your time to get the attention you need, you'll waste less energy on maintaining your barriers. Instead of running on empty you can fill yourself up with good feelings.

Chapter 17

Letting Go Doesn't Mean the End of Love

When your children grow up it can be hard to let go. Here are some ideas for moving your relationship with them to a different level.

I want it to go back to how it was

My problem pages give fascinating glimpses into other people's lives. Some stories are inspirational; others are heartbreaking. Young parents write in saying, 'Since my baby was born my life's not my own'. Then mothers whose brood has gone off into the wider world ask plaintively, 'My children were my life. What do I do now they're gone?'

One day you suddenly discover your children have grown up. It sneaks up on you. Living with them every day means you take for granted the changes in their height, their attitudes and skills. Although you've recognised their triumphs like starting work or college, somehow you think things will always stay the same. But they won't.

It's sad when you get to the end of an era. At times I didn't find it all that easy (though my daughter was a great help!), but there are plenty of parents who suffer terribly and a few who happily embrace their new freedom. Most of us fall somewhere in between. Yet many women in their seventies and eighties say they enjoyed their sixties more than any other decade, so happiness after kids is possible.

Why is it hard to let go? It is because bringing up your children has been the focus of your life for so long. It's given you purpose, shaped your routine and supplied stimulation. (That might be a nice way of saying you've had a lot of rows!) But hopefully you'll have had lots of good times too: celebrations, silly moments and things you didn't think were special at the time, like cosy family evenings in front of the TV.

There's another reason why parents want to go back to how things were. If you think you didn't get it right you might wish you could have a second chance. Knowing you can't is perhaps the saddest realisation of all. Time, though, moves forward. Inexorably your children grow up and become independent adults with desires you don't share. They have sex-lives and interests that don't involve you.

What makes the change either harder or easier is your attitude. Surveys have shown that women who invest their identity in motherhood have the most difficulty. While they're bringing up the children they put less energy into other areas of life and so feel more isolated as well as hurt when their child doesn't behave exactly as they'd wish. Then, when the child leaves home, such women no longer know who they are. They're more likely to suffer depressive illnesses and practise emotional blackmail that alienates their children. Men generally focus more on their careers, so their sense of loss is probably less intense.

If you've put energy into other interests and friendships, though, you'll have more of a path to guide you. You'll retain your sense of identity and your adult children will be more likely to want to stay in touch. All this helps ease the pain of loss.

Feeling left behind can hurt. For single parents it can be particularly devastating. You may want to force your children back into the childhood mould or pretend they're not mature enough to leave it. You might make a display of feeling regretful, nostalgic, bitter, critical. . . . But still your children grow up and that means that they grow away. Here are some ways of making the transition as painless as possible for you both.

How can I fill the empty hours?

Here are three true-life stories relating how different parents handled their children leaving home. I'm talking mostly about women because traditionally men were the ones who went out to work to earn the daily bread, which means they've got routines, careers and friends beyond home and children. Even if women go out to work they're still more likely to attach a greater amount of self-esteem to hands-on parenting than men do and so may find the 'empty-nest syndrome' more challenging.

Maureen, now in her sixties, hadn't had a paid job since her children were born. Despite wanting to cling on to her youngest son she knew it wasn't fair to prevent him following his career to a town hundreds of miles away. She said straight out, 'I'm going to miss you a lot, son. Your dad'll get by OK but at first I'll find it hard without you underfoot.' (She'd always had a sense of humour.) 'I don't want to be a limpet so I'd like your help with this to make life easier for you too. How can I let you go and not be upset?'

He replied, 'You'll have my phone number. Ring me any time you like, although better not when I'm in the office unless it's a real emergency. You can come and visit and I'll be coming home to see you and my friends. In the meantime you can catch up with some of those things you always wanted to do.'

Maureen took responsibility for making her own life as fulfilling as she could. She took Women Returners' courses at a local college, where she made lots of friends, and got a part-time job until she retired. She looked around to see what facilities her area had to offer. Her new interests are rewarding and she's pleased to feel she's a more interesting companion for her husband than she was previously. She and her son are still close but in a more adult way.

Lynda, on the other hand, didn't want to let go. It wasn't so bad when her husband was alive. Even then, she scarcely ever made the quarter of an hour walk to her daughter **Ailsa**'s place, nevertheless making bitter, manipulative complaints if Ailsa didn't come and see her at least twice a week. She also rang often because she worried about Ailsa, going so far as to tell her thirty-year-old daughter she should be wearing a vest. Once Ailsa's father died Lynda suddenly wanted to make Ailsa a substitute for him. She was forever dropping in unannounced, snooping, criticising and offering unwanted 'help', baffled by her daughter's resentment. After a couple of years Ailsa made an excuse to move away rather than put up with constant interference.

Lynda now spends her time preoccupied with her health, frequently ringing Ailsa to trouble her with the latest illness. Lynda's intention is nothing short of emotional blackmail. She believes that if she's ill enough Ailsa will have to come back home to look after her. Ailsa's responded by rationing visits and phone calls, and discounting most of what her mother says. What can be the most rewarding era of parenthood has become a spiky trap. Each, of course, blames the other.

And what of **Rafe**? His wife had left him and their two children when they were twelve and eleven. He had raised the children single-handedly, working long hours to look after their needs, and spending most of his meagre free time with them, hardly having a social life until they were old enough to go out on their own. Then he found new interests and a lady friend. His kids weren't that struck on her. **Jayne** was a nice enough woman but not their 'real' mother. Once his youngest son left home Rafe had the chance to give his new relationship more attention while still making time to visit his offspring. Over the years his kids have let go of their fantasy image of their flesh-and-blood mother. Jayne's moved in with Rafe. Her kids and his now welcome their step-parent as a full member of the family.

The moral is that your children know they deserve a life of their own and they'll get it one way or another. Treating them with respect and emotional honesty is more likely to keep you close despite the many miles that may separate you. Most of all, though, once your children have left, you're once more in the centre of your own stage. What you do in that spotlight is up to you. Are you willing to reclaim your starring role?

The Wheel of Life

While you were engaged in the practicalities, delights and frustrations of being a parent, what you did with your time and how you got attention were probably decided for you, at least to some extent. Now, though, you're the captain of your own ship.

How you manage your time will dictate how you give and get the attention you want. It's true the other way around too. Given that you've only got so much energy, let's see what options you have for expending it in the most rewarding ways.

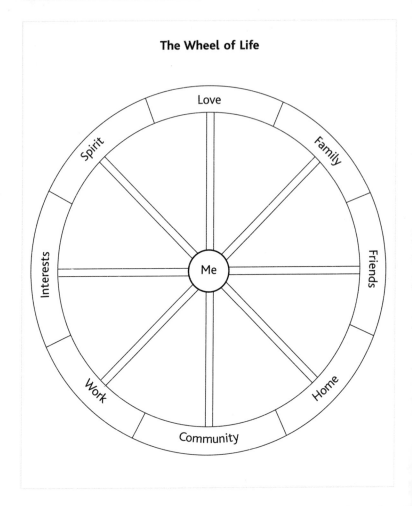

While you were actively engaged in full-time parenting, the *family* section of your Wheel of Life probably took up most of your energy. There were more chores and maintenance so your *home* section was almost certainly larger too. Now your children are off your hands, which areas could you divert your energy to instead? Which ones are most likely to get you the attention you need? Will you take up new interests and expand your friendships, or get involved in community activities so you feel valued and rooted? How about reclaiming that child's bedroom as a place for hobbies, study or to put up friends who come to stay? And what about your career? The more you put into the other areas of your Wheel, the more gets fed back into the centre. Into you, in fact.

One area that is easy to forget is *me*. If you've spent the last twenty years rushing around looking after others, the idea of spending time and energy on yourself could seem almost sinful. But it isn't. You too deserve positive strokes and love. Investing in the areas on the rim of the Wheel helps you feel good but you're allowed to nurture yourself as well.

There are plenty of ways of doing this. One is to sit quietly at ease in a place where you're not likely to be disturbed. You can close your eyes and listen to your breathing, allowing it to grow slower and deeper in the most relaxed and comfortable way. You can imagine that each in-breath is full of healing golden sunshine that spreads right through you, and that each out-breath is like a breeze blowing away troublesome negative thoughts. If thoughts pop into your mind you can let them blow away.

It takes practice. A good length of time for this is fifteen minutes daily, but it may be a while before you can make it last that long. Just centring in yourself is an antidote to stress and therefore promotes a feeling of relaxation and health. It also helps you tune in to what's going on for you.

Affirmations are another way of giving yourself feel-good strokes. They boost confidence and optimism. 'I love the way I'm living my life' gives you plenty of food for thought. Are you willing to take up that challenge? You'll find some other ways of building up your identity as an individual in your own right in the books suggested in Resources (*see page 202*).

SUMMARY

By relaxing your hold on your adult children you'll be doing them – and yourself – a favour. By shifting your attention towards making your own life as rewarding as possible, you can enjoy resuming centre stage in the story of your life. This is your much-deserved reward for all the hard work you've put in over the years. Your children will appreciate your new adult-to-adult approach and are more likely to want to keep in touch.

Part III

You and the Older Generation

Parenting is a difficult job. So is being an adult when your parents are still around. On either hand you have the pressures and delights of other adults – bosses, your partner, siblings and friends. Below you, as it were, you've got your children whose needs you're supplying. Above you are your parents, alive or dead. Now that life expectancy is greater, being the middle generation could last decades longer than it used to.

More than anyone else, parents know how to push your buttons. After all, it was living with your family that put them there. If you're lucky, your mother and father are willing to let you be an adult in your own way. They'll help you when you ask, accept your help in return, be good company when you're all in the mood and leave you in peace between times.

Even the nicest, most considerate of parents can get ill. With old age comes increasing frailty of both body and mind. If you end up taking care of your elderly parents, they may perceive it as justice – but you may feel like a slave. When one of your parents dies, the other may well look to you for support. Or you might wish they did.

On the other hand there are plenty of parents who are critical, demanding, interfering. . . . You name it, somewhere out there are well-meaning parents who are driving their adult children up the wall. And, I have to say, some parents who believe they're justified in being spiteful.

Things don't automatically ease up once your parents are dead, either. A challenging relationship with your parents will go on being difficult for some time after their demise. Partly that's a reflection of how bereavement works, and partly it's because people respond not to reality but to the version of it they carry around in their heads. If your relationship was a thorny one, mixed feelings can make it all the harder when it comes to saying goodbye. If you had a wonderful relationship with your parents, bereavement is still a rocky road.

This section, then, addresses the question of you as the middle generation, gradually shifting from being adult children to parenting your parents. My intention, as ever, isn't to criticise anyone. It's not up to me to apportion blame or praise, merely to offer choices that could make your and your parents' lives as enjoyable as possible. You're the one who's in your situation. You know how painful or how rewarding it is.

What I offer is information to help you make the best of being piggy-in-the-middle. After all, sooner or later it'll be your turn to be the oldest generation. How you model relating to your ageing parents could be how your children one day relate to you.

Nevertheless, you can also apply the techniques in this section to other situations. Whoever you're dealing with, if you want to free yourself from emotional blackmail, avoid getting stuck in repetitive rows and update your reactions to shame and blame, read on.

Chapter 18

Partners, Parents and In-laws

Here are some ways of letting go of shame and managing respect between you if there has been friction in your family between partners, parents and in-laws.

Will the in-laws like me?

Remember how you felt when you first took your new boyfriend or girlfriend home to meet your parents? What would your lover think if your father were sitting around in his vest, drinking beer and shouting at the TV? What if your mother had left her ancient knickers drying over the bath? Would your younger brother do something outrageous that would put your beloved off you forever? What if your new partner showed himself up? Do you remember that first meeting with your partners' parents that seemed so much like an interview? There was so much potential for embarrassment and shame.

Once the first meeting's over, what then? I get plenty of letters to my problem page about power struggles with parents or in-laws. Parents cut off from their son because he's with a girl (or a man) of whom they disapprove. Husbands ban in-laws from visiting and vice versa. Either of the middle-generation couple might withhold access to the grandchildren as a weapon against parents or in-laws. Repercussions can include emotional storms, legal battles, moving far away and even violence. All this misery and shame can echo down to affect generations yet unborn. So how can you and your partner form a good relationship with your parents and his? In other words, how can you let go of transference and outdated expectations?

Expectations and transference

Everyone has some preconceptions. Rather than having to work out each individual relationship from scratch, your brain, like everyone else's, stores some kind of blueprint of what it's going to be like.

That's one of the reasons for all that nervousness. When you were growing up you acted on the belief that your parents had the right to judge you. You know that your parents will be judging your new partner. Do they approve of his style, his attitudes, his career? Will he take good care of their precious child? It's the same for your partner – and your parents. Each actor in this drama is probably wondering nervously how the mass of judgements will affect the future.

All this is about transference. When you were a child your parents supplied the adult thinking until you were old enough to develop your own. They were the ones who taught you their ideas on what was good and bad. Until you truly separated out from them, their negative judgements really did have the power to hurt you because they were a part of who you were. Unless you've updated it, part of your relationship blueprint is about transferring into current interactions your old childhood idea that others can judge and punish you. Shame is believing you're not worthy. That you deserve punishment and can expect ridicule and rejection if you let anyone close enough to 'find out' what you fear is the dreadful truth about you.

Now you're an adult. Although most adults want to be liked, they know they can survive other people's dislike. If either your own or your partner's parents disapprove of you, it may not be comfortable but you can still exist, still carry on with your life, still have friends and interests and loves of your own. As an adult you're allowed your own tastes and your judgement is what shapes the way you live. But you don't always feel like that.

Some expectations, of course, are about a different kind of blueprint. Some middle-generation couples find their elders embarrassing. Financially successful people may be ashamed that their parents come from a poor background. Traditionalists might not be happy about 'letting' their eighty-year-old widowed mother who is in a wheelchair go off on the hippie trail to

Katmandu. This is about transference too: about fearing other people's judgement.

So what if your parents grew up in a tenement? It doesn't mean there's anything wrong with them. They fit into their own society and that's good enough. Why shouldn't competent adults enjoy their retirement in their own, non-traditional way? The days of pipe and slippers or knitting in rocking chairs have given way to more exciting challenges. So long as they're not hurting other people, your parents are allowed to be who they are. It doesn't reflect on you. You're separate, remember?

Greed can be another factor. You may be afraid that your parents will 'squander' the money you expect to inherit. Any solicitor will tell you that legacies can cause terrible problems between family members. But if your parents have earned the money, aren't they entitled to enjoy spending it? So long as they leave enough to cover the cost of their funeral and any debts they may have, why shouldn't they have a good time while they can? If they decide to leave you anything else, isn't that a gift rather than something you should expect?

The problem is that money can be interpreted as a symbol of love. If you don't feel secure in your parents' affections, you may want them to leave you their money as a sign that they did love you after all. If this is the case, it helps to remember that your lovableness doesn't depend on your parents' actions. How they treat you is their choice and their responsibility. Rather than taking it personally, why not bear in mind that how you treat the people you choose to be close to is a far better indication of how lovable you are? Don't you deserve your own love whether others are good to you or not?

Transference and shame

You may remember **Matt** and **Kate** from Chapter 3 (*see page 28*). Kate was caught up in a struggle to be the perfect wife and mother in an attempt to earn approval from both her husband and her mother. She learned that she didn't have to believe in outdated family rules and that by being assertive she minimised confrontation. Here's husband Matt's story.

Matt was also engaged in a subconscious fight, this time for his father's approval. In Matt's eyes he would have won this if his father phoned or visited off his own bat. Matt's father, though, had always been distant. He had a medium-level drink problem. Although he functioned well in his executive position and was the life and soul of his cocktail-party circuit, he wasn't able to be close to his family. Matt's mother had died when he was fourteen and suddenly Matt had to do a lot of the housekeeping. His father sometimes criticised his efforts and humiliated him; at other times, full of beery bonhomie, he'd offer rough praise. Most likely, though, he'd take everything for granted and leave Matt to it while he slept off his excesses or went out with his golfing cronies.

Matt's response to this was to do even more to try and win his father's love. He did well at school, graduated with a first-class degree and worked hard at an excellent job. He chose a beautiful and talented wife, Kate, and fathered two lovely children. But still his father didn't bother to make contact, and the one New Year he did accept an invitation to come and stay he was clearly ill at ease and looking for excuses to leave Matt's house.

Matt responded by extending his view of the need to be perfect to get his father's love. He now stretched it by adding Kate's and the children's behaviour and the state of the house to the reasons why his father didn't keep in touch. That's why Matt had been so critical towards his family and had often taken Kate's mother's side. Because his response was an emotional one based on an irrational belief (I/we have to be perfect to be loved), he couldn't always find a logical reply in arguments with Kate or the children so he'd walk off. Later he'd feel ashamed of his scathing remarks to Kate and wounded by her retaliatory comments. On an unconscious level Matt believed that getting close to someone was unsafe because he wasn't good enough. Besides, he thought the other person would always leave him anyway. After all, his mother had died and left him, and his father was so distant that Matt felt abandoned.

While it was true that the children were naughty sometimes and the house wasn't always immaculate, Matt's home was a normal one inhabited by normal, lovable people. But Matt's view had less to do with what was really going on than with the fact that his personal boundary had open spots. Therapists might say he had an open gestalt. In other words, part of the boundary around his psyche was like a raw wound that wouldn't heal. You can see that his boundary between himself, Kate and the kids was diffuse, hence his transferral of the responsibility for his father's indifference on to their behaviour.

Likewise Matt still carried the shame and humiliation that his father had heaped upon him in drunken moments, so he believed he couldn't feel all right about himself until he'd won his father's approval. Nor did he want to get mixed up in Kate's squabbles with her mother. For one thing – projecting his own feelings on to her – he didn't want Kate to be abandoned by her mother. On top of that he sided with a lot of Kate's mother's criticisms. Matt had transferred to his wife his father's apparent belief that people are lovable for what they do rather than for who they are.

Letting go of shame

If shame is an everyday part of your relationship with your partner, parents or in-laws, if you're afraid you'll be rejected because you're scared you're inadequate, then you too may be looking for a positive way forward. Here's what worked for Matt. Could it work for you too?

Check your beliefs against reality

Looking closely at painful beliefs about yourself can be deeply disturbing. On your own you may go round and round the same cycle and come to the same hurtful conclusions. Nobody can see their own blind spots. Otherwise they wouldn't be blind spots, would they? That's why it can be very useful to check your beliefs against reality with the support of someone you trust. That could be a partner, a friend or a counsellor. Other family members may be unwilling to look at what happened because they too are scared of what they might find, or they may share your blind spots. The earlier chapters can also help your reality checking.

Move from facts to interpretation to feelings

Looking at facts and behaviours is your first step to finding out how you've been interpreting them. It's helpful to examine how the person you've had a problem with relates to others, too. Usually the ideas can be updated to find a new interpretation that allows each person in the drama their own responsibility for what they did. This helps you put in appropriate boundaries.

Imagine you're an impartial observer back in your family of origin, say a reporter or someone making a fly-on-the-wall documentary. What picture would you form of how your parents behaved? Here's what Matt found.

Matt came to see that his father was emotionally absent not just with him but with everyone. His father had also alternated between indifference and blamefulness towards Matt's mother when she was alive. He used drink to cut off from his feelings. Rows between his father and Matt's late mother had often been about this isolation. He had never once said he loved either of them. Even with his cronies, his father wasn't emotionally open but stuck to neutral subjects like golf and office politics. This wasn't about blame but fact. The problem, then, didn't lie with Matt but with what his father did. Matt was OK. He accepted this in theory but on an emotional level was unconvinced.

Kate also presented Matt with an up-to-date reflection of his performance. She was proud he was a high flier. Matt could take this in to some extent because it was about achievements he could see. Kate then told Matt how lovable he was. He felt very uncomfortable hearing this because it confronted the inner beliefs about himself that he'd pencilled in during childhood and then inked over after his mother had died. Although he gingerly accepted the hug Kate offered he soon pulled away because he didn't believe he deserved her love. He said angrily, 'Don't lie to me! If I'm so damned lovable, how come you call me all those names every time we have a row?'

At this point Kate might have retaliated but bravely she didn't. She emphasised that she loved him very much, which was why she was so hurt when he wouldn't listen to her feelings during arguments. To her it seemed that he was withholding his love. When he stomped off she believed he was taking his love away altogether. She hurled invectives at him because that seemed to be the only thing she could use to bridge the distance she felt he'd put between them: if he too felt hurt, perhaps they could stay together to comfort each other. But when he went out of the door her further insults were just a childish way of getting back at him. In tears, she apologised and told him again how much she loved him.

Matt started crying too, and reached out to comfort her. I was very moved by this emotional moment. With other couples I might have left to give them some privacy, but part of the problem was that Matt didn't believe he could show his feelings and maintain contact, so I stayed.

Put your new beliefs about yourself into words

Matt now formed positive statements about himself. He found 'I'm lovable for who I am' to be the most important statement. He could reinforce this with memories of Kate and the children showing their love for him, and the party his friends had thrown for his birthday.

Transfigured, Matt went on to a new discovery: that sometimes you can't please your parents so you might as well please yourself. Since Matt and Kate were ethical people they acted in good faith. This also let Kate off the hook because Matt now saw that her mother was unlikely to offer praise to her daughter anyway.

Accepting that he might not get the answers he hoped for, Matt now determined to say something to his father about how he felt and what he wanted. I could hardly wait for the next session to see how he'd got on. Matt seemed happier but a little hard-edged when they came back. He sat beside Kate, holding her hand as he told his story.

Having rehearsed his conversation with Kate, he'd rung his father. Although his father had tried to head the conversation into superficial channels, Matt had said bluntly, 'I just need to know whether you love me, Dad.' After a stunned silence his father had said coldly, 'Of course I do. What a stupid question!' and hung up. Matt had written to his father, asking him to come and have a drink with him. His father hadn't replied.

'To be honest, I didn't really expect him to,' Matt said ruefully. 'I'll keep in touch with him like I always have and drop in for a round of golf every now and then, but I can't expect Dad to change the habit of a lifetime. It's his loss, not ours. But at least I know now that he loves me in his own way. That's such a weight off my back!'

No longer having to check his worth against the impossible task of winning his father's praise, Matt's life-long shame had more or less disappeared. It would resurface from time to time in moments of stress but it no longer governed his every waking action. Letting go of shame helped Kate and Matt know they were together on the same side.

SUMMARY

Now you're an adult you can survive without other people's approval. You can relax the grip of expectations by accepting your good qualities and knowing you don't have to be perfect because no one else is. To minimise shame you can check your beliefs against reality, moving from facts to interpretation to feeling. It's helpful to do this with someone you trust because they'll see your blind spots. You can take in positive data and update your view of yourself. This helps you put in safe personal boundaries too. The results are increased self-esteem and better relationships.

Chapter 19

The Balance of Power

If you've ever felt that your parents dominate your life, here are some useful ideas about getting more rewarding contact while avoiding manipulation.

What do they want now?

It was Friday night. Forty-eight-year-old **Maggie** felt the familiar twinge of pain in her chest as she got off the bus. All she wanted was to go home and put her feet up. But she was scared. Her loving husband **H** would be there to welcome her. Maggie would have looked forward to their plans for the weekend – if she'd dared. Her twins would be home from university and she really wanted to spend some time with them.

But she stood at the top of her road, reluctant to go home. It had happened all too often. Just about every Friday night for the past four years, in fact. No sooner had she got in than the phone would ring. Either it would be her sister **Maeve** complaining about their mother's latest antics, or it would be her mother whingeing about Maeve. Time after time, Maggie would have to abandon her family plans and go haring a hundred miles to London to sort things out between them. It was too much.

Eventually the cold got to Maggie. Shivering, she walked down the road and put her key in the door. 'Just this once let them be all right,' she prayed. 'They promised they could get by just this once without me.' But inside, there was H on the phone, radiating fury. 'It's your sister,' he said, holding the phone as if he wanted to strangle it, and the sinking feeling inside Maggie told her exactly what he meant.

Do you recognise this scenario? Could you write the script from memory? If you too have felt the rip of divided loyalties, maybe some of the ideas below could help.

Duty, love and loyalties

Duty is a word laden with meaning. It's what's due to somebody from you. 'Surely,' you reason, 'after all the sacrifices my parents made for me, don't I have to repay the debt they're calling in? They took care of me when I couldn't look after myself. Now it's my turn to look after them. But is having some time with my own family too much to ask? Don't I owe them something too? And why do I feel so guilty if I don't rush over to Mum's straight away?' This is more or less what Maggie said in her first counselling session. A neat woman with a frown overlaying her laughter lines, she perched on the edge of her seat as though she'd have to dash off at any moment.

As soon as the words were out of her mouth, though, she added, 'You must think I'm horrible, heartless, that I don't love my mother. I really do. She was a wonderful mother when we were little. But she causes so much trouble! Since Dad passed away she's been living with my sister and she's driving her mad. Maeve's husband **Graham is** having an affair because he can't cope with Mum being there all the time and Maeve's so angry she can hardly bring herself to speak to Mum. And now I've got angina because I'm so stressed but they still want me to go down there and patch things up between them. My husband's fed up too. He's never got on with Mum, so either I have to leave him and go down on my own, or I take him with me and he just seethes the whole time he's there. He wants me to stop seeing them altogether. I hardly get to see my girls and they'll be leaving home altogether soon. But I can hardly abandon my mum and my sister has to put up with her all the time so it's not fair to her if I don't help. What can I do?'

Poor Maggie. Poor Maeve. Poor all of them, in fact, even the mother. None of them had wanted this. But this was what they had to deal with.

The mother wasn't an awful woman. She'd lived for her children and adored her husband, but now he'd gone. She was depressed and hated being on her own. Despite medication she was agitated if no one was around. At the time it had seemed like such a good idea to pool resources so she, Maeve and Graham could buy a nice house in the suburbs. As they didn't have children it was only logical.

Unfortunately, it had meant all of them tearing up their roots. Graham still had pals in the city whom he could see before catching the train back. But Maeve and her mother hardly knew anyone. Graham came home later and later, saying he'd gone for a drink with this mate or that. Some of them seemed to wear lipstick and perfume, though, and it clung to his clothes. Social services had found a day centre that the mother could go to but she'd refused, saying she wouldn't be sent off like a schoolgirl with her dinner money to a place that was full of 'old people'. After that 'the social' washed their hands of her.

In theory, the mother did the housework, but in practice she made a poor fist of it. Maeve would come home tired from work but the place was a mess and there was nothing for dinner. Her mother didn't seem to know where the day had gone. Maeve picked up the pieces because Graham was never there. And the mother made such a fuss if her daughter didn't come straight home that Maeve didn't think it was worth going out.

Small wonder that Maeve was full of resentment. Most of all she was bitter that her mother wouldn't pull her weight and made constant emotional demands, bursting into tears or exercising her advanced emotional blackmail skills as soon as Maeve tried to do something for herself. They had terrible rows. The mother's core argument was, 'Don't I deserve your love after all I've done for you?' while Maeve's theme went, 'Whatever I do for you is never enough.' Gratitude is an ill-fitting shoe. If you wear it too long it pinches. Their behaviour pattern was repetitive. Without quite knowing how they got there, both of them kept feeling 'back to square one'. Despite their apologies and good intentions, both felt bad about themselves. Locked in this cycle, they'd call in Maggie, who also went through the same bad feelings over and over again.

If you feel a familiar discomfort as you read this, you can find a healthy way out of these repeating patterns. Here's how it worked for Maggie, Maeve and their mother.

The Drama Triangle

Understanding the Drama Triangle helped Maggie understand what was going on so she could update her strategies for dealing with it. If you watch soap operas you'll be familiar with all this. It happens at every level of society.

In any interaction between two people that is based on manipulation, there are three possible positions in which you might find yourself, as in the diagram below. Both people may compete for one of the positions, but once one of them has won that position the other has to move to another position. This goes on as long as the interaction is based on manipulation rather than assertiveness.

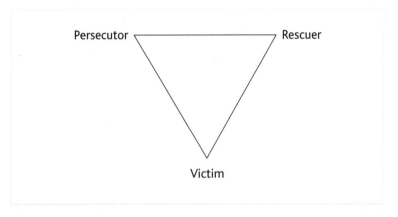

Maggie discovered that a lot of her interactions with her mother were based on this model. What would happen is that she'd receive that anguished phone call. If her mother was feeling unhappy and helpless, she operated from the Victim position, looking to Maggie to be the Rescuer and sort things out. Her usual plea was for Maggie to take her away from Maeve's home for 'a few days', which would turn into months. As her mother continued this manipulative behaviour, Maggie's daughters and husband hated the guilt-trips and rows, which happened when the mother got into Persecutor mode, criticising Maggie and her family and saying they weren't doing enough to stop her feeling lonely. Maggie went from Rescuer to Victim and then timidly suggest to her mother that it was time to go home. More arguments. It was only when Maggie finally lost her temper that she could 'get rid of' her mother. Now Maggie found herself in the Persecutor role and felt guilty while her mother renewed her helpless Victim patterns. To feel better about herself, Maggie would step back into the Rescuer role and the cycle would begin again. Maggie realised she went around separate but similar triangles with her sister and to a lesser extent with her own family. Her mother and Maeve, of course, followed Drama Triangles of their own.

Closer to home you may recognise that you too have been an actor in your own Drama Triangle. Can you see any examples of this in the last argument you had at home? The positive advantage is that you get strong emotions from each of the roles. When you're the Rescuer you may enjoy being the strong, helpful one. In Persecutor mode you may be full of righteous indignation that lets you feel like the good guy. In the Victim role you may feel bad about yourself but believe your pain and helplessness will get you Rescued so you have a ray of hope.

It seems to me that you can also have a personal Drama Triangle that may lock into interpersonal ones. Maggie would feel bad that she hadn't done enough to help her mother and sister. She Persecuted herself with guilt (and so became her own Victim) with the intention of resolving her bad feelings by doing more to help. In the early stages of helping she felt validated because she'd Rescued herself. Then, as her mother's behaviour became more hostile, Maggie would Persecute herself for getting into this mess again.

Each of the positions on the Drama Triangle also gives painful messages to you and other participants.

- In the **Victim** position, you show that you believe you're not good enough and the other person has the power to Rescue or Persecute you. You display passivity and helplessness. You act as though you have no rights and the other person has them all. You expect others to meet your needs.

- In **Rescuer** mode you'll feel superior to the helpless Victim and good about yourself. You may feel noble for putting others first, but underneath is the belief that the one you're caring for has all the rights and you have none. It's easy to martyr yourself this way – but it hurts.
- As a **Persecutor** you may feel indignant and powerful. People who bite back anger often feel quite good when they finally let themselves unleash their feelings. For the time being you consider that your own needs are paramount. You treat the other person as though they're unimportant and have no rights. But underneath is the belief that you're not valid and neither is the other person.

None of these positions is assertive. They all rest on old, mistaken beliefs about yourself and your position in the world. They're all either aggressive or passive because they lack respect for yourself and the other. They involve emotional dishonesty and their payoff is pain. You unconsciously keep going through the same repetitive stages without using your full adult resources so you end up feeling misunderstood, confused and stuck. Worst of all, you don't really solve anything.

If you're going around a Drama Triangle with someone else you do get some pretty potent contact. You're involved not in intimacy, but in a power struggle – a manipulation. If you recognise this, you can do something different to get a better outcome.

Stepping off the Drama Triangle
Here are some of the things you can try.

Operate from mutual respect
In order to accept that she and her family were allowed to do something different, Maggie permitted herself to realise that all of them deserved something better. She made a conscious effort to value herself as a competent, caring and lovable wife, mother and sister. She acknowledged that her sister was equally valuable and capable. Her mother's lovable aspect was real but without her husband to reflect it back to her it was currently hidden underneath her manipulations.

Identify what needs to be changed

The problems were that the mother no longer had the father to show her she was lovable, that Graham's infidelity had undermined Maeve's self-belief and that Maggie was exhausted. What they needed was plenty of positive emotional contact, but none of them was currently able to supply a constant stream of it.

Acknowledge your feelings and share them if appropriate

Maggie acknowledged her right to her feelings. This meant taking account of her stress and letting herself rest. Maeve needed space and other sources of positive strokes. Meanwhile their mother could learn to accept an unpalatable truth: her daughters couldn't fill her husband's place, not because they didn't love her but because they weren't him. She needed attention from the outside world too.

Use all your resources to act on your feelings

Maggie arranged a way to phone Maeve privately. First she empathised with her sister's frustration. Once Maeve felt heard, Maggie said she was sorry she couldn't do more to help relieve the pressure but the doctor had told her she needed to slow down for a while. Maggie asked, 'How would you feel if we could get Mum to make some friends so she wouldn't be so dependent on you?' Then they discussed ways of doing it. It would mean some emotional discomfort but they agreed they were experiencing that already so they had nothing to lose.

Having arranged time off and sorted things out with the day centre, Maggie came down to her sister's for a few days. She and Maeve took their rather suspicious mother on an outing, having told her that a person from social services wanted to speak to her. Their mother's fear of the authorities made her go along with this. The head of the day centre welcomed them, explained she had an urgent phone call to deal with and showed them to a table in the tea room. While Maggie and Maeve went to the servery, their mother sat with a nice-looking woman in a wheelchair who started a conversation with her. Later this woman showed them around the facilities: various craft rooms, a snooker hall, gardens and so on.

The ruse worked. After a further family visit, they arranged a Ring-and-Ride bus to ferry their mother back and forth, and invited the woman in the wheelchair to drive over to their house for morning coffee with her. Their mother started taking care of the house to impress her new friend, who also introduced her to a church with various activities. Gradually, she felt happier and cut down on her medication. Although Maeve and her mother still had arguments, they were fewer and Maeve slowly reclaimed her own life. Maggie even told her mother she wasn't well. The result was not agitation but concern. The dreaded Friday night phone calls more or less stopped and Maggie breathed a sigh of relief.

Other assertive tactics

In this instance the mother's anxiety about authority organisations like social services worked in everyone's favour as it helped her to push herself through the fear of the unknown to a better place. That's not always the case. The assertiveness techniques throughout this book could help you put in safe boundaries. After all, the longer you Rescue someone, the more disempowered and dependent they become, and it's not helpful for either of you.

Sometimes, though, for your own good, you might choose to put some distance between you and a manipulative relative. The assertive way of doing this is to explain briefly why, perhaps giving a time when you'll be back in touch to allay anxiety. Emotional Literacy gives you the tools to do this without blame.

SUMMARY

If you've been stuck in a repeating pattern of feelings and actions, has it got you anywhere? Everyone sometimes goes around the Drama Triangle from Victim to Rescuer to Persecutor, but you can use all your new-found resources to start doing something different. You're allowed to respect yourself and other people equally. With competent adults you're not responsible for their feelings, thinking or actions. It's important to acknowledge your own feelings and share them with relevant competent adults. You can act on them using all your resources, including outside help.

Once you start doing something different, even just valuing yourself, the other person can't treat you exactly the same as they had in the past. It's possible that you'll have to go through a period of discomfort while you adjust. If the person you are Rescuing is basically competent, it's important to encourage them to manage as independently as possible so you and they can step off the Drama Triangle.

Chapter 20

Relationship Games and Family Splits

You may be torn between a partner and parents – here are some positive ways forward.

I'm not having her in my house!

Family splits can be incredibly hurtful. In the 1920s a widow told her son that if he 'married beneath him' he'd be dead to his family. From the wedding until he died fifty years later, not even his cousins would speak to him. He only found out his mother had died from a newspaper. Yet his long marriage was happy and prosperous, which just goes to show that class bigotry isn't a reflection of real life.

Fortunately, fewer prejudices stand in the way today. But there are other reasons for hurtful estrangements, as you may know to your cost. Like H from Chapter 19 (*see page 166*), the person who wants to enforce the break usually has a positive intention, however painful the results. You'll see more of selfish reasons and how to combat them in a minute. But first let's look at positive intentions and see if there's a healthier way to achieve them.

'It's for your own good!'

H's intention in threatening to stop Maggie seeing her mother and sister was caring. If he'd carried out his threat, though, she'd have been under more strain, not less. Apart from the obvious pressures, he'd have been discounting Maggie's ability to solve problems. No one likes being belittled. Luckily when Maggie stepped off the Drama Triangle she averted this tearing of her loyalties.

Like H, you may want to protect your partner from family damage. If your urge to protect him discounts his feelings or abilities, why not ask him if he finds it hurtful? Could you pool your resources and reach a more respectful solution? Will you accept that the people you dislike are important to your loved one? You don't have to like them and they don't have to like you. It may not be comfortable but you'll survive. Why not find out what your loved one sees in them? No one is all good or all bad. You could tell your loved one tactfully which aspects of her family you find threatening but what she does about it is up to her. Couldn't you respect her choice? You might go easy on the criticism because you could end up carrying the blame.

There are, however, more sinister reasons for family splits. If you've felt the pain of divided loyalties, could there be a real threat to your well-being?

Disrespectful reasons for breaking contact

Two cautionary real-life stories spring to mind. Each illustrates selfish reasons for parents or partners enforcing a break of contact. You can see the results for yourself. It's worth noting that the aim of the game is shown in the final payoff. If you find yourself in a painful repeating pattern, you can work out how you get there by examining the payoff.

David was enmeshed with his parents. Although they objected loudly he married a woman he loved. A tug of war began to see whether wife **Amy** or his parents would win 'possession' of him. Without asking Amy, David gave his parents a key to the home he'd bought with his own savings near theirs.

Amy objected to her mother-in-law nosing around the place. When his wife provided evidence of this snooping, David was appalled – but not with his mother. He believed that love meant no secrets, and in his view it was Amy who was unloving because she protested. Fierce multi-handed rows ensued. David and his parents believed Amy – 'the interloper' – had no right to interfere in 'family matters'. When things came to a showdown, both Amy and his parents said David had to choose between them. While he vacillated Amy decided she didn't want to be married to three people so she left. The resulting divorce cost a fortune in money and heartache.

The more people take out their bitterness with legal battles, the greater the hurt – and the lawyers' profits. David had to sell his house to pay court expenses and the settlement so he moved back to his parents' home. He now took their selfish and misguided view that his normal, loving wife had been a harpy gold-digger and he was better off without her. Of course, he became his parents' full-time caretaker, which was exactly what they'd wanted. He believed the drudgery saved him the 'inevitable' heartbreak of further relationships. For over thirty years he didn't live his own life but theirs. Discounting his abilities, he thought separating from his parents meant unavoidable disaster. Now they're dead, he's lonely and without purpose.

There's no hope in David's story, only a dreadful warning about selfish reasons for family splits. I hope you'll acknowledge your feelings and resources and take responsibility for your own life. There's a big difference between being kind and being a doormat.

But it's the story of **Val** that offers both hope and a chance to understand how power games are played out so you have choices. Here's how Val broke free of the struggle to control her life.

Trapped in emotional blackmail

Val had always felt unworthy as her perfectionist parents offered more criticism than affection. She moved out as soon as she could, clinging to any man who showed her attention. She was heartbroken when her first three relationships soured and convinced that she deserved poor treatment. Struggling to bring up baby **Duncan** alone, she fell hook, line and sinker for **Rob.** He swept her off her feet with romantic attentions, though between times he'd often leave her waiting tearfully for the phone to ring.

Val's parents were even more critical of Rob than they had been of her previous boyfriends. She discounted the protective nature of their trenchant remarks by telling herself, 'They just don't like seeing me happy.' Now he was living with Val, though, Rob dropped his good guy act. He got drunk and violent, and was unreliable, a gambler and a spendthrift. As the Irish say, 'Angel in the street, Devil in the house.' Aware that Val's parents would see through his 'charming' act, he played on her dislike of them so he could continue to use her as source of attention, care, sex and money. 'I'm the one who loves you,' he'd say. 'I'm sad when they make you unhappy. Won't you stay away from them for my sake?' His manipulations strengthened her fear of their criticism so she cut off from her parents almost completely.

Ending emotional blackmail

Rob had been using emotional blackmail to win 'possession' of Val for his own selfish ends. David's parents had been manipulating him and Amy to gain his attentions exclusively for themselves. You could counter similar pressures.

Emotional blackmail is a plea for Rescue. That capital R reminds you that it's OK to help a competent adult if that's your choice. But if the main reason you're doing it is to feel more worthy or lovable, that's neither honest nor assertive. And it's not going to work! You and the other person are likely to end up seething with painful emotions. Partners and parents are well placed to know which buttons to press. They can use your feelings for their own purposes *if you let them*. You may not know how you've got there but you'll recognise the confusion and hurt.

At times all of us play relationship games. Once you know about them, though, you can make different choices. That way you can have healthier, more rewarding relationships with other people – but most of all, with yourself.

Your prime concern is your safety. You can't always stand up to bullying or guilt trips straight away. Any shame isn't yours but belongs to the one who's abusing you. You may have to go along with your aggressor's wishes until you can reach a safe place or get help.

Here are some ways in which you can counter the various types of manipulation. The key is to acknowledge your right to your own feelings and act assertively on them.

Make the borders of responsibility clear

Your feelings are there to protect you. If you don't like what's going on, you could say something like, 'I'm sorry you've got a problem but I can't help you right now,' or 'I'm sorry you're upset but I don't feel comfortable with what's happening. Let's talk about it later.' This isn't apology but sympathy. It can give you time to work out what you want. You don't have to accept blame that isn't yours.

If someone threatens to harm themselves to make you do something, why not call their relatives or a doctor? Whatever you do, a person who's really determined to kill himself will find a way to do so sooner or later. What he does is not your fault – it's his choice. You might say, 'That's your decision,' and walk away. If you let someone get away with emotional blackmail he'll keep on doing it to you.

Be assertive rather than acting helpless
If someone genuinely can't do something, it's fine to help out. But if you keep feeling used, why not set limits? You could say, 'I'll help you this once but after that you'll have to do it yourself or get someone else to help.' And mean it! Waiting on people hand and foot takes away their motivation to be independent so you're making a rod for your own back. Alternatively, you could act even more pathetic than they are, defer your help or make an excuse. If it's you who've been constantly looking for help or emotional Rescue, haven't you noticed you're alienating other people? Asking openly for what you want gives you the best chance of getting it.

Only ask for help if you want it
Perhaps someone keeps asking you for help but rejects all your suggestions. This isn't about solving problems. It's a ploy to keep in contact with you. When you give up trying to help, you feel frustrated and inadequate while the other person feels confused and abandoned. What she is really after is a sympathetic listener. It's your call whether to be one. If you suspect you've been using this manipulation yourself, there's nothing wrong with a short wallow in self-pity. Then you can take responsibility for fixing your problem. It's perfectly acceptable to say, 'I'm feeling lonely right now. Have you got time for a chat?'

Being a 'magic wand' invites martyrdom
Trying to be a universal fixer of other people's problems might be a manipulation to earn approval. But no one can ever be

grateful enough for long enough to make you feel good about yourself. Instead, you probably feel used. This ploy opens you up to other people's 'Yes, but . . .' games. If you're not respectful of other people's wishes and abilities, you'll probably be rejected as interfering. Your job is to fix your own life. Let other people be adults too!

Ask, don't mind read

Both sexes play this game, but women have generally been brought up to practise it more. You try to please the other person by guessing what he wants – but often he won't show you the attention you were seeking and you'll feel rejected. If you guessed wrong he may feel smothered or criticised, or just not like what you did. It's not your job to 'make' other adults happy. You can ask openly for what you want and so can he. If you want a hug you can say you do. Affection you get by asking counts double because he's honoured your wishes and you get the hug as well.

Don't fall for empty promises

If you've already said you don't want to do what the other person asks, your reasons are still valid however much she wheedles. Your gut instinct will tell you (if experience hasn't) whether or not it's a con. If you let yourself be duped into giving in and she doesn't come through with her end of the bargain, don't you feel foolish for being suckered? Empty promises may keep you in contact with someone in the short term, but your pay-off will be anger and contempt. Instead, why not say calmly, 'No, thanks, I'd really rather not'? If you're not sure you can say this directly, say that you'll think about it and give them a decision later. Or you can make an excuse and leave.

Bullying and yelling damage both parties

Bullying someone into doing something against her will shows you're giving her the power over your happiness. It's disrespectful of both of you. It may work in the short term but it sets up bad feelings. Resentment, violence and eventual rejection are the usual outcomes. Emotional bullying can include 'not speaking' until you give in. Bullies who've learned they can get away with it will escalate their unpleasant tactics. Abusive people like Rob and like David's parents (*see page 175*) usually set up for their victim to be isolated so their nastiness goes undiluted and unchallenged. You don't have to believe anything a bully says. It's only a weapon to hurt you. Find evidence to counter it and talk to other people about what's happening.

Again, your safety is paramount. If you're not safe, find a way of getting out of the situation and seek help. If it's not dangerous to do so, you can say, 'I don't like what you're doing. Will you please speak to me quietly/come home when you say you will?' or whatever specific you need to ask for.

The Results

Val couldn't apply these principles until she was willing to stop being manipulated. Only after a friend accidentally discovered how abusive Val's home-life was did Val turn to counselling for help. As she built up her self-esteem and strengthened her personal boundaries, she stopped being ashamed of Rob's behaviour and no longer took responsibility for his feelings and actions, including his aggression. In other words she *made the borders of responsibility clear.* She could decide for herself what contact she wanted with her parents and didn't have to accept criticisms she didn't think were justified. She could have friends if she wanted to.

Val rejected her self-imposed role of *magic wand*. It didn't matter that Rob *acted helpess and pathetic*, or *asked for help he wouldn't take*. Discovering that she couldn't fix him so he'd treat her well, she stopped trying. Nor had her walking-on-eggshells policy of trying to *mind read* his wishes brought her anything but grief. She decided she deserved good love and Rob couldn't give her that.

Now she found a flat for herself and little Duncan. Rob came round and slashed his wrists in front of the boy to force her to come back. This dramatic guilt trip only deepened her contempt for Rob. She called an ambulance and the police. Later, Rob began to *bully* her by making telephone calls full of *empty promises* that turned to threats. Having recorded them on her answer machine, Val got an injunction against him and asked the phone company to bar calls from his landline and mobile.

Rob eventually moved on to his next victim and left Val in peace. She's re-established contact with her parents on her own terms, drip-feeding them with snippets of information to let them know why she left Rob. Instead of the criticism she'd feared, they were in fact welcoming and supportive. By behaving assertively with them she's discovered they loved her all along.

If you want to counter emotional blackmail, here is a list of the techniques you can apply.

- Make the borders of responsibility clear.
- Be assertive rather than acting helpless.
- Only ask for help if you want it.
- Don't be a 'magic wand' – it invites martyrdom.
- Ask, don't mind read.
- Don't fall for empty promises.
- Don't bully and yell – it damages both parties.

SUMMARY

Emotional manipulations damage your self-respect and your relationships. By acting assertively on all your feelings you give yourself power to resist. It's your choice how much contact you have with emotional blackmailers, and what kinds of contact you'll accept.

Chapter 21

Caring, Bad Feelings and Empathy

If the demands of your elderly parents have been leaving you resentful, here are some ways to release your anger safely and find empathy for them.

Caring is wearing!

Around 5 per cent of the population will find itself caring to some degree for elderly relatives. Simultaneously rewarding and frustrating, being a carer evokes powerful emotions like love, duty, resentment and guilt. It spells a period of increasing restrictions and demands as well as a new relationship with someone you used to know in a different capacity. This may last for years. Fear can also play a part: if the parents who once seemed so powerful and eternal can disintegrate, what of you?

If you've ever felt bad about the demands your dependant relatives impose on you, here are some ways to counteract uncomfortable feelings so you can find compassion and hope.

I feel terrible!

Tom was visibly upset when I saw him. He's a nice man in his fifties, a little chubby and grey around the temples but smart in his business suit and tie. His wife **Gilda** was a nursery nurse and adored working with children, especially since their own had now grown up and moved away. Tom's parents lived sixty miles away. He loved them dearly and Gilda was fond of them too.

When Tom's mother died suddenly his dad **Roger** went rapidly downhill. Roger lost his appetite and, with it, his strength. Worst of all was his depression. He couldn't see the point in going on and gradually shrank in on himself, prey now to infections.

Tom tried everything. Invitations to stay met with refusal. He arranged for a bereavement counsellor to visit, but Roger called her an interfering busybody and shut the door in her face. He would not speak to the vicar. He never let Meals on Wheels in, so they stopped coming. The hospital tests Tom arranged showed there was no phsyical reason for his father's dramatic weight loss.

The worried Tom came twice a week to tend his father's garden, collect his pension and do his shopping. Gilda cleaned the place and cooked tasty meals to tempt the old chap, bringing him enough fresh and frozen meals to last him for the rest of the week. Time and again they showed him how to use the microwave they'd bought him, but Roger couldn't be bothered with it, and he wouldn't use the cooker. Eventually Gilda discovered that all the food she prepared so lovingly was being dumped like rubbish.

Roger's old friends stopped coming to see him because he plainly saw them as a nuisance. He wouldn't join in family outings or celebrations but retreated into himself, rarely stirring from his chair by the TV. He was losing track of time and behaving erratically. Gilda called in the doctor who prescribed anti-depressants, but Roger only pretended to take them.

Coming out of the bathroom one chilly spring day, Roger had a fall. The pain of two broken ribs stunned him. When he regained consciousness, moving hurt too much. He never carried the alarm his son had bought for him and the phone was downstairs. He didn't call out for his neighbour because he didn't want to 'make a fuss'. So he lay on the landing, growing colder and stiffer. It was only when he didn't answer Tom's nightly phone call that anyone realised something was wrong.

Tom and Gilda drove too fast through the frosty darkness. They found Roger unconscious and breathing noisily. In a fever of anxiety Tom called an ambulance. The paramedics said Roger had hypothermia and bronchitis as well as the broken ribs. Gilda felt that the staff in the emergency room were giving them suspicious looks, but Tom said she was imagining it – until a medic questioned them in such a way that it was obvious the possibility of neglect and cruelty hung in the air. Fortunately, Tom was able to say that his father's doctor would confirm they'd often called him in.

For a fortnight Roger recuperated in hospital. He put on weight and started taking something of an interest in his fellow patients. The hospital would only release him if Tom and Gilda had to him stay, which they'd already said was their intention. The occupational therapist came several times, encouraging Roger to be active and independent.

Outwardly, Roger went along with this. No sooner had he arrived at his son's place, however, than he wanted to go back home. He complained about the food, said the weather was too hot or too cold, didn't want to get up and then refused to go to bed. He wouldn't set foot outside the door, not even to enjoy the garden as summer drew on. Feeling helpless as his father's condition deteriorated, Tom eventually took Roger back to his home but made sure that the lady next door would look in when Tom and Gilda couldn't. The Citizens Advice Bureau helped them to arrange an attendance allowance payment for the helpful neighbour.

That autumn, bronchitis and a stroke left Roger frailer than ever. His periods of dementia were longer lasting and more profound. It was obvious he was hardly taking care of himself at all. Now Tom and Gilda had to make choices: to give up their lives and move in with Roger, have him stay with them or put him in a home.

They chose to have him stay with them. That meant Gilda giving up work because they couldn't leave him alone. But Roger now treated them as though they were jailers. He had tantrums rather than eating in front of them. The doctor encouraged them to be firm and fair as with a child. Roger was agitated and tearful, doing the same senseless things over and over again. His sleeping patterns were disordered and he'd cry out, so their nights were often disturbed.

Sometimes Roger didn't recognise them. Not liking the sound of his voice after the stroke, he wouldn't speak to them. Nor would he use the picture book of common objects he'd been given so he could communicate. He didn't like going to the respite centre and sometimes when the ambulance came for him he'd make dull screaming noises or take off all his clothes, although he was perfectly happy (and stayed dressed!) once he got there. Roger's feelings, then, were bewilderment, resentment, agitation and depression. But what of Tom and Gilda, and how would you feel if you were in their shoes?

Bad feelings and ways to manage them

Tom and Gilda were torn. They could remember Roger as he had been: Tom's cheerful, capable father. But this shrunken, crochety old man didn't even look like him. They were annoyed that their lives had been so drastically curtailed, and hurt that their kindness was rejected. They felt inadequate because nothing they did made any real difference.

Gilda missed the stimulation of work and colleagues. She hated the smell of the commode and was angry that Roger wouldn't always use it when he needed to. All his extra washing exhausted her and she damaged her back trying to help him out of the bath. She was horrifed that Roger kept groping her, and absolutely furious when he put his hand up her daughter's skirt. After that Tom and Gilda's children helped out reluctantly but didn't really like visiting. Gilda resented that, too.

Guilt also played a big part in their feelings, not least since Roger bruised so easily and they were scared someone might think they'd been abusing him. Each felt the most hard done by: Tom because he'd lost his father and Gilda because it wasn't even her own flesh and blood. Without Gilda's income they were struggling financially, but the old man hadn't made a will and now wasn't mentally competent to do so. Putting Roger in a home was beyond their means right now. His house was crumbling, but the legal process before they could sell it might take years. Meanwhile Tom's estranged half-sister turned up from South Africa accusing them of trying to cut her out of her inheritance and maltreating her father. Taking her to the lawyer and the doctor helped, as did leaving her to take care of her father for a day.

It was hardly surprising that Tom experienced one further feeling which disgusted him: he sometimes wanted his father to die. 'After all,' murmured a small part of him, 'Dad's got no quality of life and while he's here we can't enjoy ours either.' This thought damaged his self-esteem. When he eventually confessed it to Gilda, she whispered that she felt the same. That was some consolation but not much. Forgetting that his wife had also made choices, Tom now felt guilty for putting this burden on her.

Age Concern and Help the Aged were very useful, as was the Citizens Advice Bureau. These and other resources are listed at the back of the book (*see pages 204–5*) if you need to get in touch with them. Keeping in contact with the doctor and social services is also important. But what of those negative feelings? How could Tom and Gilda deal with them?

Fear

Just because one of your relatives has dementia, it doesn't mean that you will. The more active you are mentally, physically and socially, the less chance there is that you'll develop it. A varied diet plus mineral and vitamin supplements are also thought to combat its possible onset.

Anger and resentment

It helps to understand that the person with dementia isn't being awkward on purpose. He can't help it. It's true that there might be an element of game playing in his behaviour, but it's not from his adult awareness. No one wants to feel confused and agitated. His mood swings, even anger and violence, don't necessarily have a malicious intent and he may not realise he's just hit you.

It's also important to detach emotionally from a person with dementia. This doesn't mean you stop loving or caring for them but if you start to feel distressed or angry, you can either do something physical or engage your thinking instead. Step off the Drama Triangle! You don't have to believe abuse or accept inappropriate sexual contact. You can seek help. You're entitled to it.

Anger releases adrenaline, which can build up until you feel ready to explode. Exercise helps burn it off, even if it's only dancing around the kitchen. If you do get time to yourself, you could stand under a railway bridge or in the middle of a field and shout. Hopefully you have an understanding friend with whom you can share your feelings. If anyone offers criticism of your anger, why not invite them to care for your dependant for a time?

Studies have shown that listening to comedy tapes or canned laughter for around half an hour daily can lift your mood and help combat depression even in stuck situations. What you think, do and feel can all help you find some moments of pleasure. Why not make a list of available, inexpensive treats such as a bubble bath or a video? Crafts, study and other home interests are useful. If you can arrange a break even for a couple of hours you'll feel well-earned relief. It's important to keep up your social life as far as possible. You can phone friends or invite them round. Religious leaders may agree to find volunteers to give you some temporary respite, and social services or hospital day centres offer other alternatives.

Guilt and shame

Your dependant's condition is not your fault. It's not catching and you don't need to be ashamed of anyone seeing him. Nor are you to blame if you experience negative feelings towards him. It's not comfortable but it is normal. Feelings are not actions. So long as you do your utmost to treat him with care and respect you're doing all that anyone could ask of you. Any inappropriate sexual advances aren't directed at you personally, but at some character or memory inside his head. It helps to laugh them off if you can. Nor are you responsible for how he feels. If he's tearful or agitated you can calm him sympathetically, but you don't have to share his feelings. Caring for a dependant is heroic and people in society value that.

Sadness

It *is* sad to see someone you love disappearing piecemeal. You've lost someone who's dear to you and the dwindling shell of him can't make up for that. This is known as pre-grieving. There's more about managing grief successfully in the next chapter.

You'll probably also have lost various opportunities of your own, at least for the time being. But you'll be able to make other opportunities for yourself eventually. It's helpful not to show you're upset in front of your dependant because he'll become distressed. Masking your sadness with anger damages you and those around you. It's all right to share your sorrow with people who can understand. The Princess Royal Trust for Carers has an online chatroom you might like to join.

Hopelessness

If you look at your whole future at once you're likely to see it as an unhappy continuation of your present difficulties. It helps to focus on making the most of your opportunities now, however limited they may seem at first sight. The future with all its rich possibilities will still be there. Providing you keep as optimistic as you can, there's no reason you shouldn't enjoy the rest of your life.

Lack of compassion

Caring for somebody *is* compassionate. You don't have to feel pity or love for this shell of a person, or anything else you believe is 'good'. But you do have to treat your dependant with care and respect. Apart from anything else, if you don't, you'll damage your own self-esteem. And how you treat your elderly dependant may be the model for how your relatives care for you when you're old.

Two exercises can help. The first is a simple one. Gather mementoes of more positive days to share with your dependant. Reminiscing together helps you renew your good feelings about him. I agree it gets boring to hear the same half-remembered anecdotes over and over again, but these are things he treasures and they help him recall his identity and worth. You might chip in with happy stories of your own.

The second exercise is called *unifying*. It's also good if you've had an argument with someone. Sit down comfortably, close your eyes and contact in your imagination all the nice things about who you are, what makes you your own special self. Friends, lovers, skills, happy times. Use all your senses to make your memories vivid: how the wind blew sand into the picnic that day on the beach, how the sun felt on your skin, the tang of the sea breeze and the taste of ice-cream, what you felt paddling in the cool waves, the laughter of family and friends, and other sounds you heard. Choose from among your happiest memories, although imaginary scenes could help if you're finding it hard to recall feeling good. If you can, include cheerful times with your dependant when you were both younger.

Once you have some clear images using all five senses (sight, sound, touch, taste, smell), put yourself in your dependant's place and see life through his eyes. He too will have had experiences

like these (which you've probably heard about time after time!).
He too knew sunshine and laughter, work and friendship and
love. Once he skipped and sledged and played football. You and
he inhabit separate bodies at different stages of health, but the
core of your experiences is the same and comes through the same
five senses.

What would it be like to be trapped in a failing body without
your usual clarity of mind? How would you like to be treated?
Along with nourishment, safety and shelter, wouldn't you want
love, respect and dignity? If you devote ten or twenty minutes to
this exercise you'll probably feel happier in yourself and much
more compassionate.

The Results

Tom was glad he'd got things off his chest, and relieved to find
his feelings were normal. So was Gilda. Both found the unifying
exercise particularly helpful. By concentrating on making their
present as rewarding as they could they built up hope for the
future. Wanting to be happy wasn't selfish but an ordinary human
trait. As they acted assertively on their feelings they found more
pleasure, which is the greatest antidote to stress. This helped
confirm their personal identity. They found it easier to tolerate
the daily frustrations of caring for Roger, which translated into
having more patience and even some good times with him.

When Roger's father finally passed away, Tom and Gilda felt
genuine sorrow as well as relief. Both of them agreed that although
it had been hard, the experience had helped them find inner
resources they might not otherwise have discovered. By acting as
helpmates as well as lovers and friends, they deepened their affection for each other. They also felt, quite rightly, that they'd earned
the right to happiness and could value it all the more.

SUMMARY

Caring for a dependant, elderly or otherwise, is challenging. By
acknowledging your feelings and addressing them assertively you
can enrich your life despite the difficulties. Elderly dependants
deserve care and respect. So do you! You can get help if you
need it.

Chapter 22

Healing Grief and Relaunching Your Life

If you've suffered a bereavement, could you use some ways to start healing your pain?

How can life have meaning without him?

A new widow once asked the late Queen Mother about bereavement. 'Does it get any better?' she said. The Queen Mother replied, 'No, but you get better at it.'

Sooner or later everyone experiences the agony of loss because death is the healthy and inevitable conclusion to life. If it's someone close you're likely to experience a jumble of emotions. These take time to work through. The widowed say that on average it takes between eighteen months and two years before they come out of that dark place, but as you saw with Roger in the last chapter, some people get trapped in grief for much longer. Here are some ways to heal the heartache.

The reality of loss

When someone you love has died, you experience a real loss. If the deceased was important to you but you've had conflicting feelings about her, the loss can be more complicated, as we'll see shortly. Let's not forget those people like Tom, whose father survived for some years but not as himself.

There can be a big difference between what you've actually lost and your perception of your loss. I often hear widows say, 'I feel as though I don't exist without him', or 'Without him life has no meaning'. At first this may seem true. Particularly if the person who's passed away is a beloved parent, the child – even the adult child – may feel lost in a place for which they have no map.

This is partly because the deceased formed a big part of the survivor's world. His opinions gave guidance. Even if you rebelled against them, you decided that his beliefs told you what *not* to do. Without him your world has changed shape. If it was a parent who was good to you, you've lost their protection and support. Whether loving or not, you have in a way lost a buffer between you and death because now you're in the oldest generation.

The one who lives on no longer has her loved one to reflect her existence and lovableness any more. At this point the bereaved person may genuinely feel that she doesn't, or shouldn't, exist. It can seem as though one person + one person = one person and if either of you dies there's nobody left at all.

However, even when your loved one was alive you existed independently. You had friends, skills and interests. Your senses told you of pleasure and pain, which you experienced through your own body. Even after your loss you still have these things. Like every other person on the planet you're entitled to live and to make the best of your life.

It's true that you've lost the physical companionship of the person who's died. This doesn't mean, though, that you can't take pleasure in other companions. I know it's not the same but you can still chat, go out, enjoy your interests and go on holiday.

Some people think that recovering from grief is disloyal. They believe that laughing or just carrying on living is a sign that they didn't love the person they've lost. It's not true. If you've believed this up to now, you may be shocked to hear that recovery is a far more accurate indicator of a good relationship. Close relationships are emotionally honest and respectful. Your loss will therefore be deeper but you'll feel strong enough to let yourself experience it fully so that you go more directly through the pain and rebuild your life with a new place in it for your loved one's memory. You'll also have friends to support you and you'll know you're allowed to share your feelings.

Letting go of your grief isn't the same as forgetting. Being as happy as you can in the present is a tribute to the love you've had in the past. If you need help, you can talk to a bereavement counsellor. Organisations like Cruse are there to support you when you're ready. (*See* Resources, *page 203*)

If your loved one was ill before she died, you may find that sad images of her overlie the happier ones. But this was only one phase of her life and being her carer was only one phase of yours. They don't cancel out the good times or take away all the wonderful things you shared. It can help to carry around a photo of your beloved as you'd like to remember her: smiling, vital and loving. Nobody can take those shining memories away. Celebrating your loved one's life is important to her and to you. I know this can be hard to do, but don't you think it would be a betrayal of all she meant if you stopped treasuring the good things you've been lucky enough to share?

It's strange but true that when someone you love dies, it completes your relationship with them, rounds it off and makes it possible to find a positive new way of looking at what you had, at yourself and at the world. Before we see how working through the four tasks of mourning can help you find comfort, I'd like to explore one other aspect of loss.

Complicated loss

A friend who's recently been bereaved didn't shed a tear at her father's funeral. She only went to see him well and truly buried. Seeing the grave filled in was the proof she needed that he could never hurt her or anyone else again.

This is more common than you might think. If you've felt this way you've probably kept it to yourself for fear that people who don't know the facts will judge you. But you're not alone. Many children of neglectful, cruel or abusive parents feel a surge of relief when they hear they're finally safe. They do feel a great loss, though. They've never had a loving father who nurtured them and kept them safe and now they never will.

My friend has allowed me to tell you a little about her experience. I feel both honoured and privileged to share this with you. I know there are hundreds of thousands of people who've gone through the same thing. Each individual's story is different but there's a common thread uniting them.

My friend can't remember a time when terror didn't rule the home she grew up in. Her father would attack her mother, who was utterly cowed by his aggression. He'd also beat the children. The mother later claimed she'd had no idea her husband sexually abused several, but possibly not all, of his children. She was too damaged and too scared to stick up for them.

Some of the girls actually accepted their father's advances in order to protect their little sisters. The atmosphere of secrecy and threat meant no one in the family would talk about what was happening so each carried their own sense of shame. Some even tried to deny what they'd gone through. This was understandable but because no outsider ever shone a light into that hellish darkness the survivors never realised that the shame and the guilt weren't theirs but their father's.

Small wonder, then, that there are people who grow up hating the abusive parents they had and desperately missing the loving parents they should have had. If this strikes a chord with you, I am glad that you have survived and I honour whatever you had to do in order to stay alive. I repeat that the shame isn't yours. It rightfully belongs to the one(s) who abused you. You can get help. Even if all this happened decades ago you can find comfort and recovery in telephone or face-to-face counselling. Counsellors won't judge or condemn you but will be accepting and supportive. They can help you lay your guilty secret to rest so you can find confidence and peace of mind.

Your experience of the deceased may not have been that polarised. Probably most bereaved people have some conflicting feelings. Partly this could be about circumstances – relief the deceased is no longer suffering, for example – and partly it could be because of a complex relationship. Nobody is all good or bad but if you made painful decisions about yourself in response to your childhood experience of that person, you may feel hurt, angry, betrayed, sad, regretful, triumphant and guilty all at once. If you've worked through the first part of this book, hopefully you're starting to let go of some of the pain, but here are some other ways of moving forward.

The tasks of mourning

Mourning has been a part of existence since the dawn of humankind. It has four phases. Each phase can support you through the other phases. People tend to cycle through them, revisiting each phase until its task is completed, but sometimes people get stuck in one of them so that their misery is prolonged or turns to depression. The same phases are likely to happen if your loved one stops being herself during her lifetime (pre-grieving), and again when she passes away.

Since part of the emotional turmoil of bereavement is a feeling of being all at sea, you can help yourself find your way if you understand what's happening for you. The four phases are as follows.

Acceptance

Working towards accepting your loss takes time. It's normal to go through a period of numbness when you're first bereaved. This is the body's way of helping you get accustomed to your loss. The practicalities and problems of organising the funeral can help keep your mind off your pain. You may feel confused and bewildered, sometimes forgetting that your loved one is dead. When you remember you're likely to feel guilty and then sad all over again.

You may go through a period where you can't settle down to anything and keep finding you're going through your handbag or your pockets; only after a while do you realise you're actually looking for the person you've lost. If this agitation goes on for more than a couple of weeks it's important to talk to your doctor about it. It's worth asking yourself whether it's intended as a manipulation to 'make' your loved one come back to you or to get attention from your relatives. Neither of these are healthy positions. Full acceptance comes gradually if you allow it to.

Anger and guilt

Few people will admit it but anger is a common component of bereavement. You may be angry at your loved one for dying and abandoning you even if you know he didn't want to go. Many people are also angry with the loved one for actions and decisions he took during his lifetime. This can include financial ones that have implications for you now he's dead. An unfocused rage against the universe is also common, so you may find yourself unreasonably cross if the postman whistles as he comes up the path. You may be furious with officials or mail-order companies who keep sending letters addressed to the deceased. It's common to feel angry with people who haven't been bereaved. For a time you may be angry with your God for letting your loved one die, but eventually your faith usually comforts you once more.

Given that some people are uncomfortable dealing with anyone who's been bereaved, you may also be livid that some friends avoid you for a while. It's hard not to feel doubly abandoned in this situation but it can help to know that it's not personal. You can feel sorry for them because they have such limited emotional skill – but you don't need to tell them that!

If your loved one died in hospital you may be angry with medical staff for not keeping him alive. Most people also turn their anger in on themselves and feel guilty. This could be because your thoughts follow the *if only* trail: 'If only I'd done this instead of that she'd still be alive', or 'If only we hadn't had that silly quarrel he'd at least have died happier'. As much as 99 per cent of all *if only's* aren't reality based. If trained medical staff couldn't keep your loved one alive, how could you have done?

The others, the sharp words or small acts of everyday unkindness, were just a little part of your relationship. The person who died had also been at fault sometimes and you responded to that. The rest of your relationship will have been compounded of many neutral things and some good ones.

Forgiveness is for your benefit, so you don't keep anger burning through your veins like molten lava. You might want to consult a religious leader, or write a letter to the person you've lost in which you express your outrage, hurt and loss. You could make it as vengeful as you like to start with, and then as time goes by write gentler versions where you recognise that the person may not have been able to help acting the way she did. You can make a ceremony of destroying these letters so they don't hurt future generations – or hurt you any longer, either.

Putting things in perspective helps. As ever, healthy exercise helps defuse anger. Sorting out practical things helps the healing process, but please don't throw away everything that belonged to the deceased. You may regret it later.

Part of this clearing out process could be the urge to move house. However, making big decisions while you're still in the throes of grief often leads to distress. While familiar surroundings may remind you of your loved one or his death, moving will mean you're also losing your community and routines. You'll be further from your friends and not necessarily confident enough to make new ones straight away.

Sorrow

Sadness is a natural reaction to losing someone you loved. Sometimes, though, people are so scared the sadness will drown them like a tidal wave that they're unwilling to face it. Then they're likely to get stuck in the acceptance or anger phases. While they don't experience the full depth of their sorrow they can't work through it and so are likely to feel vulnerable and tearful until they decide to start moving forward. One of the functions of a funeral is to 'lance the boil', as it were, by beginning to share your grief with others.

Talking about your loved one is important. Others will probably be reluctant to start conversations about him because they don't want to upset you. This doesn't mean they don't care or they're not sad themselves. You can ask if they mind you bringing up the subject yourself. You can reassure them that tears don't mean you're going to pieces. This way they'll know when you're ready. You may feel hurt if they're not ready to talk about him when you are, but it's not a rejection of him or of you. Perhaps they're not ready to contact their grief. Sometimes people need to hold themselves together for a while before they can let themselves feel their own sorrow.

Eventually, though, your sadness will fade if you let it, though anniversaries may renew it for a time. It helps to know your loved one would want you to be happy.

Rebuilding your life with a new place in it for your loved one's memory

You'll probably be facing a series of new challenges in daily living. If it's a parent you've lost you may automatically reach for the phone to tell him of your triumphs or seek his advice. I know I still sometimes think, 'Oh, I'll ask Dad about that', and my father's been dead for ten years. But you have to learn to manage without that particular loved one. Even practical problems like managing your bank account or getting the shopping home could mean finding new solutions. On the positive side handling all this is good for your confidence.

While the experiences you shared moved into the past even when he was alive, they're still in your memory, even without his physical presence. I like to think of memories as a sort of gallery in which I place treasured images in a golden spotlight.

It's worth asking yourself if there are ways in which your life is richer because you've known the person you've lost. How could you pass on what you've learned from being with him? How might other people benefit from it? Would he be proud of the way you're managing; the way you're honouring the gifts he's given you of freedom or choices? Do you want to celebrate his living or his demise?

Your life, though, is your own. Whatever you've received, how you treat it is up to you. I wish you the confidence to move forward to new joys. They'll stand out more clearly against the shadows of your grief.

SUMMARY

I sympathise with your loss. Recovering from grief is an accolade to your strength and to the love you shared with the person you lost. You can rebuild your life and find new happiness if you let yourself. I hope you do.

A Final Word – Branching Out

The journey through this book has opened areas of darkness and of light. All along, the destination has been to discover the delights of life inside and beyond the family – in other words, how to be the person you've always wanted to be. For each of us, the map of how to get there has been different because in some senses we've all begun from our own unique starting place. Yet there are common factors: a home, either individual or communal; a set of beliefs we can update or not; and the opportunity to reach out to our fellow travellers if we choose to.

I invite you now to view your life as a journey. You can grow towards either happiness or sorrow. You can either improve the scenes through which you pass or not. Even if you've had a rough start in life, you can build something better. As Buddhists say, 'The deeper the mud, the more beautiful the lotus.' You can move on, knowing you're the only real arbiter of whether you live a good life. It seems to me that by treating the companions you meet along the way with as much respect as you reasonably can, you'll get back as much as is humanly possible. You'll earn friendship and love; you'll minimise heartache; you'll have greater confidence and far more fun.

I hope you find the ideas in this book help you to free yourself from old hurts and build a brighter life for yourself and those around you.

Resources

FURTHER READING

NLP: The New Technology of Achievement, ed. S. Andreas and C. Faulkner, Nicholas Breasley, 1996

Are You the One for Me?, Barbara de Angelis, HarperCollins, reprinted 1998

The Hyperactive Child, what the family can do, Belinda Barnes and Irene Colquhoun, Penguin, 1984

How to Enjoy Your Life and Your Job, Dale Carnegie, Vermilion, reprinted 1998

The Love Laws, Steven Carter, Piatkus, 2001

A Woman in Your Own Right, Anne Dickson, Quartet, 1982

Wonderful Ways to Be a Stepparent, Judy Ford and Anna Chase, Conan Press, 1996

Toxic Parents: overcoming their hurtful legacy and reclaiming your life, Dr Susan Forward (with Craig Buck), Bantam, 1990

Creative Visualisation, Shakti Gawain, New World Library, 1995

Men Are from Mars, Women Are from Venus, John Gray, HarperCollins, 1993

Feel the Fear and Do It Anyway, Susan Jeffers, Century Hutchinson, 1987

Assert Yourself, Gael Lindenfield, Self-Help Associates, 1986

The Positive Woman, Gael Lindenfield, Thorsons/HarperCollins, 1992

Emotional Confidence, Gael Lindenfield, Thorsons/HarperCollins, 1997

How to Talk to Anyone, Leil Lowndes, Thorsons, 1999

Diary of a Teenage Health Freak (teen sex education), Aidan MacFarlane, Anna McPherson and John Allstrop, Oxford University Press, 2002

Women Who Love Too Much (and the men who love them), Robin Norwood, Arrow, 1986

The Celestine Prophecy, James Redfield, Bantam, reprinted 1996

The Confidence to Be Yourself, Brian Roet, Piatkus, 1999
Families and How to Survive Them, Robin Skynner and John
   Cleese, Mandarin, 1983
Life and How to Survive It, Robin Skynner and John Cleese,
   Mandarin, 1993
Intelligent Emotion, Frances Wilkes, Arrow, 1998

This section is largely for the reference of professionals, but may
be of interest to other readers.

NLP: The Technology of Achievement, ed. S. Andreas and C. Faulkner,
   Nicholas Breasley, London, 1996
Basic Family Therapy, Philip Barker, Blackwell Scientific
   Publications, Oxford, 1992
Principles of Group Treatment, Eric Berne, Oxford University
   Press, 1966
What Do You Say After You Say Hello?, Eric Berne, Grove Press,
   NY, 1972
The Feeling Good Handbook, Dr David Burns, Plume/Penguin, 1990
The Racket System, R. Erskine and M. Zalcman, Transactional
   Analysis Journal, vol. 9, 1, 1979
Injunctions, Decisions and Redecisions, R. Goulding and M.
   Goulding, Transactional Analysis Journal, vol. 6, 1, 1976
The Structure of Magic II, John Grinder and Richard Bandler,
   Science and Behavior Books, California, 1976
*Structural Diagrams of the Personality Adaptations Correlated with the
   Quadrants,* Vann Joines, Transactional Analysis Journal, vol.
   18, p. 188, inspired by Kaplan, Capace and Clyde, 1984
Personality Adaptations, Vann Joines and Ian Stewart, Lifespace
   Publishing, Nottingham, 2002
Process Therapy in Brief, Taibi Kahler, Little Rock: Human
   Development Publications, 1979
Conjoint Family Therapy, Virginia Satir, Souvenir Press, London,
   1978
The New Peoplemaking, Virginia Satir, Science and Behavior
   Books, California, 1988 www.avanta.net, the Virginia Satir
   Network
Scripts People Live, Claude Steiner, Grove Press, NY, 1974

TA Today, Ian Stewart and Vann Joines, Lifespace Publishing, Nottingham, 1987

Transactional Analysis Counselling in Action, Ian Stewart, Sage, 1989

Developing Transactional Analysis Counselling, Ian Stewart, Sage, 1996

Personality Adaptations, Paul Ware, Transactional Analysis Journal, vol. 13, 1, 1983

Affirmations: injunctions, permission and redecision, Mark Widdowson, TA UK 58, Autumn 2000

The Passionate Technique, Antony Williams, Tavistock/Routledge, London, 1989

The Maturation Process and the Facilitating Environment, D. W. Winnicott, Hogarth Press, London, 1960, reprinted Karnac Books 1995

Momma and the Meaning of Life, Irvin D. Yalom, Piatkus, London, 2000

HELPFUL CASSETTES

Are You the One for Me? Barbara de Angelis, Audio Renaissance, 1992

Loving Affirmations for Achieving and Maintaining Optimum Health, Louise Hayes, Hay House Audio, 1990

Meditations with Shakti Gawain (series of 4), Airlift Book Company, London

Emotional Intelligence, Daniel Goleman, Thorsons Audio, 1997

Emotional Confidence, Gael Lindenfield, Thorsons Audio, 1997

Supreme Self-Confidence (VHS video), Paul McKenna, New Hypnotherapy Series, Rank, 1999

HELPFUL ORGANISATIONS

These include useful websites. Phone numbers are for the UK where local branches can be found through Directory Enquiries.

General

My pages: www.emotionalmagic.net

www.lineone.net/lifestyle/agonyaunt/askanne.html

www.parentsonline.gov.uk

UK Asian Women's Centre: 0121 523 4910
Families Need Fathers: www.fnf.org.uk
MIND (mental health charity): 020 8519 2122
Phab (Physically Handicapped-Able Bodied): 020 8667 9443
Samaritans: 08457 909090

Abuse, physical/emotional

Bullying: www.dfes.gov.uk/bullying; www.bullying.co.uk
SAFE (addresses domestic violence including towards men):
www.dgp.utoronto/ca/~jade/safe/index.html
www.womensaid.org.uk
Childline: 0800 1111
Incest Survivors: 01224 211079, www.siaswso.org
MOVE (Men Overcoming Violence): 0161 434 7484
Parentline (for parents under stress): 0808 800 2222
Rape Crisis, central UK: 020 7916 5466
www.self-injury.info
Women's Aid: 0117 977 1888

Abuse, substance

www.alcoholics-anonymous.org
Alcoholics Anonymous: 0121 212 0111
Al-Anon, the support group for families of problem drinkers,
can be reached through the AA number above.
Aquarius (alcohol-related problems): 0121 632 4727
Families Anonymous (for friends and families of substance
users): 020 7498 4680, www.familiesanonymous.org
Lifeline (for substance users and their families): 0800 716701

Advice

Citizens Advice Bureau: www.citizensadvice.org.uk

Aged

Age Concern: www.ageconcern.org.uk
Help the Aged: www.helptheaged.org.uk

Bereavement

http://griefnet.org

Cruse: 0870 167 1677
www.miscarriage.org.nz

Carers
The Princess Royal Trust for Carers: www.carers.org
Department of Health site for carers: www.doh.gov.uk/carers

Counselling organisations
Institute of Transactional Analysis: www.ita.org.uk
admin@ita.org.uk (to find nearest Transactional Analysis
counsellors)
British Association of Counselling and Psychotherapy:
www.bacp.co.uk
UKCP (United Kingdom Council for Psychotherapy):
020 7436 3002, www.psychotherapy.org.uk
Your GP may also be able to refer you to a counsellor

Gambling related problems
Gamblers Anonymous: 08700 50 88 80

Gender and sexuality related questions
London Lesbian and Gay Switchboard: www.llgs.org.uk
www.gender.org.uk
Beaumont Society (Transvestism/Transexuality): 01582 412220
(UK)
Gay Switchboard: 0121 622 6589

Health
Attention Deficit and Hyperactivity Disorder: www.adhd.com
British Dyslexia Association: www.bda-dyslexia.org.uk
National Autistic Society (autism and Asperger's): www.nas.org.uk
Autism helpline (Mon–Fri, 10a.m.– 4p.m.): 0845 070 4004
National Deaf Children's Society: www.ndcs.org.uk
National Eczema Society: www.eczema.org

Parenting/Stepparenting
www.parenting.com
www.parentsoup.com

www.parentlineplus.org.uk
www.stepfamily.asn.au

Relationship counselling
Relate: 0121 643 1638, www.relate.org.uk

Single Parents
Gingerbread: 0800 018 4318, www.gingerbread.org.uk

Index